PRAISE FOR

THE PASSION GAP

"Philip provides a practical guide to living one's purpose and meaning while addressing the financial reality of fulfilling them. This book is unique in its approach of combining philosophy, psychology, and finance. A great platform for parents to discuss essential life questions with their children."

—**LOREN SHUSTER,** Chief People Officer and Head of Corporate Affairs, The LEGO Group

"*The Passion Gap* is what the world has been waiting for. Though written from a father's perspective, this book can speak to anyone, at any age. Phil's ability to make the process of figuring out life is unmatched and needed more today than ever before. This book is a must-read!"

—**TERMIKA N. SMITH,** EdD, MPA, Associate Director for Policy and Communications, US Public Health Agency

"Finding purpose and happiness is a monumental task. So is finding a job in its current form amidst a fast-changing world—made more complex when we add passion into the mix. Philip lays out a step-by-step process of figuring out what is really important to us. Because if we don't forge our own path, someone else will."

—**PHILIP CARRIGAN,** CEO, Morunda

"*The Passion Gap* is beautifully written with honesty and sincerity. As a parent and mentor, I found Philip's approach of not prescribing—but of offering a perspective and way of thinking—to be one that will be most helpful to a number of people. I look forward to presenting each of the young people that I mentor a copy of Philip's book."

—**CHEW GEK KHIM,** Executive Chairman, Straits Trading Company and Tecity Group

The Passion Gap

WHAT OUR PARENTS DIDN'T TEACH US

ABOUT PURPOSE, PROSPERITY, AND

LASTING HAPPINESS

Philip F. Hsin

Some names and identifying characteristics of persons referenced in this book have been changed to protect their privacy. This book contains the author's present recollections of experiences over time. Some details and characteristics may have been changed, some events may have been compressed, and some dialogue may have been recreated.

Published by River Grove Books
Austin, TX
www.rivergrovebooks.com

Copyright © 2024 PFH Strategic Advisory Pte. Ltd.

All rights reserved.

Thank you for purchasing an authorized edition of this book and for complying with copyright law. No part of this book may be reproduced, stored in a retrieval system, or transmitted by any means, electronic, mechanical, photocopying, recording, or otherwise, without written permission from the copyright holder.

Distributed by River Grove Books

Design and composition by Greenleaf Book Group
Cover design by Ploy Siripant
Illustrations by LeValerie Singapore

Publisher's Cataloging-in-Publication data is available.

Paperback ISBN: 978-1-63299-875-0

Hardcover ISBN: 978-1-63299-940-5

eBook ISBN: 978-1-63299-876-7

First Edition

To my dearest E and S,

No matter the path you choose in life, know that I'll always be by your side.

CONTENTS

PREFACE IX

ACKNOWLEDGMENTS XIII

INTRODUCTION 1

PART 1: HAPPINESS 9

CHAPTER 1: Happiness—The Long and Short of It 11

CHAPTER 2: Finding Your North Star 31

CHAPTER 3: Money and Happiness—How Much Is Enough? 51

PART 2: INCOME 73

CHAPTER 4: What Is a Job? 75

CHAPTER 5: Income Sustainability in the New Economy 97

CHAPTER 6: The Financial Independence Mindset 125

PART 3: INTEGRATION 151

CHAPTER 7: Defining and Finding Passion 153

CHAPTER 8: Bridging the Passion Gap 173

CHAPTER 9: Finding Meaning, Purpose,
and Lasting Happiness. 195

CONCLUSION 219

NOTES 225

ABOUT THE AUTHOR 233

PREFACE

When I found out I was about to become a first-time father at 44, the first thing I did was find a therapist. Don't get me wrong—I was beyond thrilled by the news! But even as I eagerly looked forward to the arrival of my firstborn, the thought of being someone's father opened the floodgates of self-doubt. My appeal to the family therapist was simple: *Help me ensure I don't pass my emotional baggage on to my children.*

By then, I'd carried that load long and far enough, mostly without even taking stock. Let's just say there's a lot to sort through when it comes to my childhood. When I was nine, my family fled the horrors of war in Cambodia, our homeland, to resettle as refugees in a low-income neighborhood in Portland, Oregon. Well into middle age, my parents lost everything they knew and started over in a foreign land, with little money and less English—while supporting four young kids. Not too surprising, then, that they lacked the emotional bandwidth and cultural understanding to support us kids as we struggled to adjust. *Talk about heavy cargo.*

As my parents slowly rebuilt their lives, I had to reconcile the world I'd known with the new American values and beliefs around me. The United States, I was told, was "the land of opportunity." There, children are often taught to "pursue their passions" and become "anything they want to be." Instead, isolation and shame defined my childhood, fueled by a pervasive sense of falling short, which I carried well into adulthood. Now as a parent, I didn't want any of that for my son, E—or for my daughter, S, who arrived two years later. If I could just pave a less challenging path for them on their journey through life . . . but *how*?

Through my tumultuous life journey across two continents and spanning close to six decades, I had picked up some invaluable life lessons that I'd like to share with my two children. However, I knew that doing so as an older parent would be improbable—especially in passing on lessons that apply to their adult lives.

Around that time, I picked up Eugene O'Kelly's book, *Chasing Daylight*. O'Kelly had served as CEO and chairperson of KPMG US—one of the world's largest professional service firms—before developing terminal brain cancer at age 53. His memoir chronicles the approximately 100 days between that diagnosis and his untimely death. Mainly, he wrote about the importance of being happy in the present moment and the value of close relationships. What stood out for me was the legacy he left his loved ones. I was also inspired by a concept conceived by writer Bruce Feiler. When, like O'Kelly, Feiler received a serious cancer diagnosis, he recruited a handful of trusted male friends to form "a council of dads" that his daughters could always turn to for fatherly support or advice.

We've all heard it takes a village to raise a child, and I agree—though it feels theoretical at best. I grew up an outsider in a strange land, basically raising myself (and not infrequently botching the job). This idea of a fatherly council rather than an individual, struck a chord with me, reinforcing my belief that no two people share the same set of values in terms of religion, money, work, family, friendship, love, and so on.

This book serves as my legacy to my children and, in lieu of my own "council of dads," offers a guidebook of sorts to help them—and anyone else reading along—to navigate the jagged path through adult life. Not to indoctrinate anyone into my way of looking at or moving through the world, but to help others uncover their *own* values and aspirations, then align their life choices accordingly.

Unlike me, E and S have always lived in Singapore, where they were born. Still, this book deals a lot with the socioeconomic and cultural trends of the US, particularly those related to two (often contradictory) American obsessions: work and "passion." That's in part because my American upbringing shaped my struggles to reconcile prosperity and passion, and in part because the US economy and culture have a disproportionate impact on markets and societies around the globe.

Although written with my kids in mind, this is not a book meant for children. After all, I'm still here to provide age-appropriate guidance for my now 12- and 14-year-olds. Instead, I address this book primarily to the man and woman my son and daughter will someday become as they forge their own paths—both through early adulthood and in the decades to follow. My goal isn't to forecast specific details about the society or marketplace my kids will inherit, but to delve deeper—straight to the core of what matters most.

WHAT MATTERS MOST?

So . . . what *does* matter most? What universal principles or guideposts, if any, should direct each individual's passage through life? What questions can we ask to shed light on the path ahead? I don't pretend to have all the answers, but in my attempt to at least find the right questions, I've learned some things I'd love to someday share, say over an evening drink with my grown-up kids.

For now, I invite you to pull up a chair, maybe pour yourself a glass, and dig into what matters most. Questions that wiser (and more foolish) minds than mine have tackled throughout the ages: passion and prosperity, happiness, meaning, and purpose.

How do we define and achieve "success" in life? How much money is enough, how do we go about earning it, and what does "passion" have to do with anything? Most importantly, what does it take to find true meaning, purpose, and lasting joy during this fleeting time together?

I have some ideas.

ACKNOWLEDGMENTS

This book, being my very first, would not have been possible without the tremendous amount of support and encouragement that I received from my friends around the world.

I would like to first thank Philip Carrigan, Cheong Kwok Wing, Eleanor Foo, Mike Ho, Adam Khoo, Alex Khor, Samuel Kim, Elliott Maggs, and Tay Swee Yuan for granting me permission to share their stories. I learned a tremendous amount from each of them about life's priorities and about myself.

I would also like to thank Samuel Kim, Michael Stockford, and Tay Swee Yuan for being my early book reviewers. Their early input and guidance helped to shape the content and voice found in the book.

A big thank-you to Hussein Al-Baiaty, Eric Chua, Jackson Chua, Fionn Ee, Philip Jay Kim, Sang Yong Lee, Jenny Lim, Lim Siong Guan, Manuel Malabanan, Graeme Mather, Richard McLean, Paul Monk, Desmond Ng, Termika Smith, Loren Shuster, Philip Vlieghe, Meredith Wolff, Yan Uhl, Carolyn Wong, Elvire Wong, and Nicole Zhang for their generosity in taking time to read through a part of or the whole manuscript and for providing their invaluable input.

I want to also say a special thank-you to Vincent Ang, Chew Gek Khim, Dennis Koh, Cindy Lim, Tay Swee Yuan, Rosa Wang, and

Bambang Widjaja for not only helping to read and provide feedback on my manuscript, but for also always being available to speak and provide guidance when I was testing out new ideas or concepts for the book.

Of course, without the guidance of River Grove Books, who helped to take over this project at a late stage, this book would not be possible. Thank you to all the team members who made this possible.

Lastly, I need to acknowledge the general practitioner who first inspired me with his sage advice about what mattered most in life. I'm sorry that I can't thank you directly as I've lost your contact details over the two-plus decades that it took me to put your advice into this book.

INTRODUCTION

The other day, while filing documents in my home office, I found a scrap of paper filled with words (some misspelled), pictures, and dollar signs—all scribbled out in pencil. The work of a small child.

My son, E, had drawn up three options—including estimated prices—for his upcoming eighth birthday party. These ranged from a basic buffet at our condominium pool to a catered celebration at a member's club with a wave pool. Below the condo swim party option, he'd written "ok"—next to a crying, frowny face. It struck me: He'd chosen the best value for money, even though it made him sad to do so.

At first this brought a smile to my face. My son was learning good money management! But that feeling soon gave way to a tinge of guilt. I could have easily afforded the more elaborate option (and E likely knew that). Somehow he'd still weighed fiscal responsibility over his own celebration—when he was only seven years old. At that age, what could feel more joyful or indeed *important* than a birthday party?

ORIGIN

That's when I began to wonder how many of my values, justified or not, I'd already imparted on my kids—in this instance, where I might seem to correlate money with happiness . . . or perhaps value money *over* happiness itself?

Was I somehow setting up his boyhood to look like mine—even though (unlike my parents) I had the luxury of choice? Was E feeling vestiges of the deficiency I felt as a child? What if those feelings led him to overcompensate later for self-imposed restrictions, to work long hours at unfulfilling jobs, only to exaggerate "status" through reckless spending, as I had done?

In many ways, our two childhoods couldn't be more different. I grew up in a low-income Northeast Portland neighborhood, a Cambodian refugee with extremely limited resources. Sponsors from a local Lutheran church had set up my family of six in a small apartment with two bedrooms: one for my parents and one for my two sisters—my elder brother and I slept in the living room. We used meal vouchers for school lunches and wore secondhand clothes. I still remember the shame and confusion I felt when kids made fun of my "high-water" pants. New to the English language, I thought they were laughing at my hand-me-down Converse canvas high-tops—so I found scissors and cut my shoes as low as I could. This, of course, made matters worse.

My children live in stark contrast: a three-story corner terrace home in a highly desired Singapore neighborhood, their own en suite bedrooms, and branded clothes and shoes. E and his sister enjoy nutritious meals, supplemental enrichment classes—even a helper who looks after their needs.

I have achieved, by most measures, success as a finance professional. But how should we measure "success" as an adult—or as a parent? Can

I feel proud and secure passing my values and lessons on to my son and daughter? Will they continue my legacy? *Should* they?

Because here's the thing. Achieving professional success in early adulthood—I became regional director of North Asia for a global asset management firm at 33—did *not* provide me with some pervading sense of emotional well-being, nor did it provide a healthy mindset. My life focused unilaterally on work and lacked meaning or purpose—let alone passion.

Instead, my combination of childhood struggles and early career success bred a thirst to acquire. To buy and display shiny objects—the latest gadgets, branded suits, you name it. I once bought nine luxury timepieces in a two-year period. I'd chase that next dopamine rush, only to quickly lose interest and repeat the cycle—well into adulthood.

OBSESSION WITH WORK

I mentioned earlier the tension between the American work ethic and notions of "passion" and happiness. Despite the stereotype of the optimistic, smiling American, people in the US tend to work long hours, while reporting diminishing returns when it comes to life satisfaction. According to 2022 data from the Organization for Economic Co-Operation and Development (OECD), Americans outworked the Japanese by 204 hours a year, British workers by 279 hours, and German workers by 470 hours.[1]

Meanwhile, the idea of "following your passion" seems woven into the American ethos, even as most working Americans experience a distinct lack of work-related enthusiasm or drive. Most feel the need to choose between what they define as "passion" and their need or desire to earn a decent living. This incongruity is what I call the "Passion Gap," and like everything from capitalism to social media, this American trend has spread around the world.

It was only after I embarked on a multiyear search to understand how meaning, purpose, passion, and money interconnect that I began to feel some semblance of *lasting happiness*—which, for me, means simply waking up each morning with the feeling that I'm on the right path to achieving my meaning and purpose.

WHAT DOES IT MEAN TO BE HAPPY?

Why do parents give children advice? Most parents would say, "I want them to be happy."

The logical next question, of course, is, "What does it mean to be happy?"

Popular life advice has a way of reducing our multifaceted reality to quotable—if overly binary—sound bites: "Follow your *passion* and the money will come." Or the opposite: "Follow *money* because you need to be pragmatic."

These answers tend to reflect the perspectives and experiences of advice givers—but not necessarily of those on the receiving end. Shouldn't we, instead, figure out how to tailor advice to fit the unique set of values, goals, experiences, and circumstances of the individual it's meant to serve?

The Passion Gap provides an account of my journey to define and attain lasting happiness, plus important lessons related to self-exploration that I learned along the way. I began this work to someday help my own children better understand themselves so they can filter life's many lessons—including their dad's advice—through their own values and aspirations. After all, I shouldn't expect them to live up to expectations I set for myself, or those I've set for them.

Part 1 will explore different sources of happiness, how to identify the ones that last, and, finally, how happiness relates to money. We'll highlight some philosophy, psychology, and modern brain science before focusing on what matters most: our guiding core values—what I call our personal North Stars. Finally, since we can't live on values alone, we'll address the role of money as it applies to happiness.

Part 2 focuses on how we earn, beginning with how jobs have evolved over time and how to avoid common job-related traps. Next, we'll tackle how to thrive in a world with less income and job security, combined with fewer worker protections and a growing global wealth gap. A lot comes down to understanding the unique mindsets associated with traditional employment, entrepreneurship, and investing, respectively. Then, we'll delve deeper into what it takes to develop a mindset of true financial independence.

Finally, Part 3 reconciles our quest for long-term happiness with the need to earn through ideas related to passion, as well as meaning and purpose. To begin, we'll explore the nature of passion, how to identify yours—and, of course, how to bridge the gap between earning what brings you contentment and doing what you love. At that point, as we'll see in our final chapter, meaning and purpose become surprisingly easy to find—directing the path toward lasting happiness.

ROLE OF FAITH AND AUTHORITY

Before we move on, I have some disclaimers. One has to do with the role of religion and spirituality. Some people have suggested to me that God and religion should have no place in a book centrally concerned with personal and professional success. Others insist that any book asking questions about happiness, meaning, and purpose should foreground faith as a central and universal guiding force.

In the end, I've concluded that we all must find our own purpose and meaning. The key is creating and sustaining a life in alignment with our values and beliefs, whether driven by self or family, or by society or faith—or anything else greater than ourselves. There are no right or wrong answers here, just ones that work for us and ones that don't.

Finally, let's address the question of authority. Who am I, after all, to write a book about such grand themes? I am not a psychologist, philosopher, or recognized scholar. I am simply a father who deeply loves his children and asks a lot of questions.

More to the point, I am a father who wants to share his experiences searching for meaning, purpose, and prosperity (not necessarily in that order) so that his kids—and anyone else along for the ride—might benefit. I'm not prescribing any particular route for the journey. If there's one key takeaway from this book, it's this: We must all do what's right for us as individuals. Everything comes back to personal purpose and meaning, as directed by our individual North Stars. Once we've located that, finding true happiness—and bridging the Passion Gap—becomes far more attainable. This book attempts to provide tools and perspectives needed to draw your own map to get there—wherever "there" may be for you.

In other words, I may be the author of this book—and of my own life's journey—but I am not the *author*ity on anyone else's life, values, or personal choices, including those of my children.

I vividly recall one particular conversation I had with the family therapist after my kids began attending school. I was talking to her about the hunger that came from my early need to survive, and how I converted that into a drive to succeed that has served me throughout life.

"How do I instill that same drive within my children?" I asked.

Her reply? "You can't."

She calmly explained that my children will likely (*hopefully*) never have to go through the same or even remotely similar circumstances as I did. In other words, they'd never be able to see the world "through my eyes." Nor should they. Instead, she said, "Find other ways to lead them. Help them find their own drive, in light of their own lived experiences—rather than your own."

Hopefully, the approach described in this book helps motivate my children to not just survive amid the challenges of a rapidly changing world—but also thrive. I want them to understand—as early as possible—how to find and, above all, sustain happiness through serving their core values and achieving financial sustainability in a way that nurtures passion, meaning, and purpose within their lives.

I've concluded that our best bet is to know ourselves—to examine our own personal beliefs and values—then take actions aligned with those beliefs and values. If nothing else, at least this book will inspire my children (and other readers) to take that elusive first step: asking the questions in the first place. That, in my humble opinion, will determine your unique course toward bridging your Passion Gap and finding meaning, purpose, prosperity, and, ultimately, lasting happiness.

PART 1
HAPPINESS

1

HAPPINESS—THE LONG AND SHORT OF IT

Happiness is the meaning and the purpose of life,
the whole aim and end of human existence.

—Aristotle

My high school graduation aligned with the height of 1980s decadence, when big hair and baggy suits defined men's fashion. I idolized bands like Duran Duran, particularly their bassist John Taylor, who rocked a silk shirt and upturned collar like nobody's business. But let's just say that, even after my parents completed their community college courses and found more solid financial footing, brand-name clothes remained far out of reach.

The summer after my first year in college, a cousin invited me to work at his import-export business in San Francisco. I'd worked part-time jobs since age 12—picking strawberries during summer break, then washing dishes or busing tables at a Chinese restaurant—but this was a serious leveling up. All of a sudden, I could make more money than I'd ever imagined—in San Francisco, a city that embraced '80s excess. I wanted a piece of that lifestyle for myself: to look like a pop icon, to feel like I belonged, to show girls my age that I was worthy of their attention.

At the end of the summer, my cousin paid me US$2,500, and I felt like the richest guy on the planet. Instead of saving for my next semester at Portland State University, I blew the whole sum on designer clothes: shirts elegantly fitted around the shoulders, pants tailored to cascade around the ankles, a shoulder-padded jacket to mix and match with my beautiful new ensembles—even a few silk ties in subtle geometric designs I knew I'd rarely wear. For a brief moment, I felt ecstatic about my purchases. I imagined myself swaggering into a party and turning everyone's head with my new threads and air of success.

But those fantasies soon dissipated—and serious regret crept in to take their place. I'd left no money for what I needed that school year, including books for some of my classes.

Ten years on, I fell into the same trap. I was making a successful career for myself in the world of international investments: living in Hong Kong, occupying a beautiful 39th-floor office in one of the then-newest buildings overlooking the harbor. I was smitten by the flash, glamor, and in-your-face money of that very cosmopolitan city. My Canadian flatmate came from a relatively well-off family—and he dressed the part. I envied his Armani style. Certain that I'd feel more at home in my new city if I exuded similar elegance, I started collecting expensive suits and luxury watches: brand-new Cartiers and IWCs and vintage Rolexes that cost more than a decent used car. Before I knew it, I had nine watches. But just like that first summer in college, these possessions left me feeling empty.

That's when I finally realized just how misguided it was to think money could buy happiness. Not that I didn't appreciate the craftsmanship of a Rolex or the feel of a designer suit, and I certainly enjoyed lavish parties and weekend trips. But I was finally coming to terms with an underlying, unshakable discontent. During my first seven years in Asia, I worked hard and got rewarded handsomely. Still, I found myself in a job I wasn't passionate about, at a company in which I took little pride. No amount of luxury watches, expensive suits, lavish parties, and weekend getaways could compensate for the melancholy.

I had slipped into a full-on existential crisis. I didn't know who I was or what I wanted or how to live a life of meaning and purpose—let alone with passion. What I did know was that I needed to dig myself out of the muck and find real happiness for the years that remained of my life—but how?

THE HISTORY OF HAPPINESS

Ask 20 people what makes them happy, and you're bound to get as many different answers. Type "What is happiness?" into a search engine, and you'll get just over 16 billion results—yet there seems to be no one answer we can all agree on.

That hasn't stopped philosophers, theologians, and poets throughout the centuries from asking the question. I read a fascinating account of this quest by Professor Darrin McMahon of Dartmouth College. In his 2005 book, *Happiness: A History*, he explained that the concept of *happiness* originates from the Old Norse *happ*, meaning "luck" or "chance." The word was also associated with the idea of "fortune" throughout the Middle Ages and Renaissance. That makes a lot of sense to me. If you were, say, a 16th-century blacksmith toiling to support your ever-growing family, happiness might seem like a privilege reserved for "lucky" royals and aristocrats.

Looking at the history of Western civilization, one gets the impression that even *contemplating* the meaning of happiness was considered a luxury—maybe even a sin. Piety and austerity dominated the European zeitgeist for centuries. It wasn't until the 18th-century Enlightenment period that conversations really began to shift. Around 1733, English poet and thinker Alexander Pope wrote a philosophical poem claiming happiness to be "the end of all men and attainable by all." A few decades later, in 1776, America's Declaration of Independence boldly declared, "Life, Liberty, and the pursuit of Happiness" to be the unalienable rights of all people, as "endowed by their Creator."

By this time, the Industrial Revolution had begun. While industrialization didn't initially do much to expand the average person's free time—factory work was harsh, long, and sometimes even deadly—it did change how people earned and spent both their money and their free time. As the cost of consumer goods and services decreased, the average person's "pursuit of happiness" could now include evenings out on the town and acquiring more and nicer things.

Today, of course, we have a lot more leisure time to reflect on big, lofty life questions. But the irony for me is that we don't seem to be any closer to answering them than that blacksmith or factory worker hundreds of years ago—except that these days, we turn to search engines for insight.

The US has largely driven the modern global emphasis on happiness. Americans invented Happy Meals, the yellow smiley face, and

Disneyland, "the happiest place on earth." Even the American middle-class work ethic seems to center on the notion of work as a source of happiness. From an early age, we train kids to pursue big dreams for personal fulfillment: "What do you want to be when you grow up?"

However, as the global obsession with happiness grows, so do signs of cultural dissonance. We've watched as rates of depression and discontent both soar. We rely on antidepressants while flashing smiles of perfectly straight, whitened teeth. We blow money on cars, clothes, and tech gadgets while living paycheck to paycheck on credit.

Perhaps we're looking at the question all wrong. So many of us (consciously or not) equate happiness with short-term sensory indulgence: that decadent bite of chocolate, a new luxury handbag, the feeling of warm sand between our toes on some tropical beach vacation. Those are great experiences for sure, but they lack the staying power to nurture more lasting and meaningful contentment. In other words, they're what the ancient Greek philosopher Aristippus called *hedonic* sources of happiness: experiences that maximize pleasure while minimizing pain.

If you haven't heard of Aristippus (435–356 BCE), he lived during the fourth and fifth centuries BCE and studied under Socrates. He's best known for founding the Cyrenaic school of moral philosophy that deemed enjoyment of life through pleasure—sensory enjoyment not just of courtesans, fine foods, and aged wines (although certainly those) but also of each passing moment—as the highest good.

Toward the end of Aristippus's life, his school of thought came under fire by Aristotle (384–322 BCE), who instead espoused the virtues of *eudaimonic happiness*. Unlike hedonic happiness, Aristotle's version focused more on self-actualization through philosophical contemplation. This meant living according to your *daimon*, roughly translated as "character" or "virtue." Like Aristippus and other thinkers, Aristotle wondered about the ultimate purpose of human existence. He believed that while happiness was indeed that ultimate end, material wealth and sensory gratification represent mere means to that end—not ends in and of themselves. Instead, according to Aristotle, "happiness turns out to be an activity of the soul in accordance with virtue."

After I'd spent decades unhappily chasing money and pleasure, that got my attention.

In some ways, my journey reflects this mental shift from a default hedonic approach to one more consciously rooted in Aristotle's concept of *eudaimonia* as "an activity of the soul in accordance with virtue"— but as these are rather esoteric and academic terms, I prefer to call them *short-lived happiness* and *lasting happiness*. When viewed through these two lenses, we start to see why so many of us get trapped. The decision to buy a new car or suit feels easier—and certainly delivers a greater (if shorter) emotional high—compared to Aristotle's contemplative life. That is, until we realize how the pursuit of pleasure keeps us running on a treadmill, chasing a lasting joy that seems always just out of reach.

LUNCHROOM PECKING ORDER

I spent way too many years on this treadmill, starting when I was very small. When we were kids in Portland, my younger sister, F, and I had very different spending habits. Anytime we had money, I'd rush to the store to blow it all on sweets—which I'd immediately consume. F, meanwhile, always set some money aside and finished her candies slowly. I'd inevitably end up begging her to share her treats and promising to repay her. While she acquired both savings and a healthy habit of moderation, I trapped myself in a splurge-borrow cycle of my own design, always in debt and dissatisfied. Always hungry for the next sweet prize.

I'd love to say I learned better as we matured into adulthood. Instead, I repeated the mistake of pursuing short-lived happiness—replacing Red Vines licorice and chocolate-covered raisins with designer suits and luxury watches.

Upon reflection, it's clear I've been looking for happiness in all the wrong places for most of my life—growing up in Portland, that summer in San Francisco, and even as a high-achieving professional in Hong Kong. I also now see why flashy wealth-signaling objects boosted my ego. It was not just pleasure-seeking behavior, but also pain avoidance—to compensate for the years of ridicule and lack of self-worth I'd endured as my family struggled to build a new life in a foreign land.

Looking back to those early years in Portland, I learned quickly about social stratification from the hierarchy of the school lunchroom. Wealthier kids brought bright metal lunch boxes packed with fresh sandwiches and expensive snacks. Then there were kids who bought tickets for cafeteria food. Finally, there were the lunch voucher kids, stained with the stigma of financial aid.

It was embarrassing to be a lunch voucher kid. To make matters worse, someone gifted me a lunch box of my own—a shiny blue one depicting the bionic secret agent on the '70s TV series *The Six Million Dollar Man*. Each day, my mom sent that lunch box with me to school—empty. I'd stand in line with my lunch voucher in one hand and an empty lunch box in the other, feeling like some outcast imposter. Cafeteria ladies would frown at my lunch box, puzzled, then fill my plate with food and send me on my way. When I finally asked my mom about it, she told me she had assumed the lunch box was for bringing home any leftover food. We both quickly learned that was not how things worked in the States.

By high school, I'd become devoted to instant gratification. Instead of focusing on my studies, I gravitated toward friends with similar maturity deficits. We'd carouse at house parties and late-night get-togethers even as I worked three nights a week. I skipped classes and copied homework assignments from more diligent classmates. Meanwhile, I spent all my hard-earned money on clothes meant to impress young women. Attention from them ultimately led to sex—another risky and short-lived way to boost my low self-esteem. This pattern lasted well into my college years, when my grades fell to the point that I risked losing my financial aid and ended up transferring to another university—and away from the only friends I'd ever known.

A lot of this comes down to unexamined motivations. Take exercise: How many of us actually work out to nurture our health? How many instead hit the gym to make up for the internalized shame of growing up as the "skinny kid" or the "fat kid"? Your motive largely determines whether you sustain an active, healthy lifestyle or end up on steroids or diet pills.

When motivated by shame and lack of self-worth, it's much easier to take things to an extreme and completely lose perspective—not to mention balance.

THE BRAIN SCIENCE

You might assume that Aristippus—who prized short-term hedonic happiness above all else—lived a life of pure, unadulterated indulgence 24/7. In fact, he likely wasn't what we now think of when we hear the term "hedonistic." Aristippus did actually argue for things like intelligence and virtue—though not exactly out of deference to some higher good. He still saw enjoying each moment as the ultimate goal, but he understood that truly maximizing enjoyment over the course of one's life requires discernment and moderation. Otherwise, the mind and body become not only habituated and less receptive to pleasure, but also damaged and degraded by its pursuit. As we all know, too much of a good thing can quickly tip the balance from pleasure to pain, which, of course, Aristippus wished to avoid.

In other words, without knowing the modern neuroscience behind it, Aristippus understood something about the brain's reward system. When it comes to short-term happiness, our brains are ruled by the feel-good hormone, dopamine. Dopamine gets released every time we engage in a pleasant activity, whether eating our favorite food or playing with a puppy. This chemical improves our mood, creating a sense of well-being—and motivating us to do more of whatever causes it. We're literally wired to crave these sensations, so we learn early on to seek out those activities and behaviors that create them. How many children do we see today addicted to their smart devices? Their knee-jerk devotions to addictive digital activities remind me of my own weaknesses regarding first sweets, then expensive clothing and watches.

When we feel that shot of dopamine, our brains want to repeat the experience, which reinforces neural pathways, ingraining behavior into habits and even addictions—whether to alcohol and drugs, sex and pornography, food, or even exercise. We feel the urge to do something (anything!) to keep those dopamine levels elevated. This was exactly what happened when I got that US$2,500 from my cousin: I became so fixated on the short-term pleasures of fancy new threads that I completely lost sight of very real and consequential financial needs.

Before long we may find ourselves in massive debt, morbidly obese by binge eating, or chemically dependent on a substance to have fun or cope with stress. The problem, of course, is that none of these habits bring lasting happiness. At best, they mask our underlying emotional unrest and lack of direction in life. In the case of substance abuse, our brains trick us into thinking we feel great when, in fact, the alcohol or drugs only damage neural pathways and impair brain function.

For true, lasting happiness, we must understand and avoid this spiral. Choices that emphasize instant gratification set the baseline for future habits that limit our success and satisfaction. Even very high-functioning, successful people can fall prey to this. How many stories have we heard about successful businessmen, actors, musicians, and athletes who succumbed to drug or sexual addictions? Too often, these led to ruined careers and/or early deaths that left families, friends, and fans devastated and confused.

We need to combat our short-lived tendencies by practicing delayed gratification. However, undoing this dopamine-seeking loop and replacing it with healthier neural pathways is not an easy task. My realization about early childhood traumas and destructive spending impulses helped me change course toward a more balanced and healthy lifestyle. However, self-control only goes so far. We also need the right motivation.

DELAYED GRATIFICATION AND REWARD SUBSTITUTION

You've likely heard of the Stanford University Bing Nursery School marshmallow test from the early 1970s. Four- and five-year-old children were seated in front of a single marshmallow or other sugary snack, then left to wait alone with the treat—and the knowledge that if they resist the devilish pull of sugar for just 15 minutes, they can enjoy a greater reward (*more* marshmallows!).

The scientists next tracked the participants for more than 40 years. Walter Mischel, who conceived the study, reported finding that the children who managed to wait for the bigger payout were more likely to succeed in a number of areas—higher SAT scores, higher levels of self-reliance and self-confidence, not as easily distracted, and better able to cope with stress.[1]

Truth be told, while I can easily resist a marshmallow, I still have a weakness for flashy toys and impulse buys. I regularly meet for breakfast with friends, many of whom have an appreciation for life's finer things—including sports and luxury cars. But each time I fantasize about cruising down the streets in a Maserati or Ferrari, I remind myself that my enjoyment would be brief, followed by prolonged and profound regret.

To better combat the brain's weakness for short-term happiness, Dan Ariely, a professor of psychology and behavioral economics at Duke

University, suggests something called "reward substitution." Basically, it's a way to trick your brain by associating a short-term reward with activities related to a longer term goal. Ariely offered a personal example. After being hospitalized for hepatitis C, Ariely took part in an FDA clinical trial of injections intended to prevent the long-term liver damage often caused by the hepatitis C virus.

The problem was that these shots, though ultimately life-saving, caused some unpleasant short-term side effects—not to mention the discipline needed for the injection itself three times a week. To motivate himself to take his medicine, Ariely decided to link it to an activity he enjoyed: watching movies. Basically, Ariely applied to himself a form of Pavlovian conditioning. Take the shot, watch a movie—while potentially preventing a liver transplant years down the line.

While I agree that such techniques can be powerful, I wonder . . . *Can tricks like reward substitution provide enough motivation to reliably curb temptations and impulses?* Perhaps for some. The rest of us likely need something deeper and more meaningful to stay on track.

To me delayed gratification in and of itself is not enough—not if you don't know what you're doing it for. Training just for the sake of discipline as some higher good feels somehow hollow. I mean, it's certainly helpful for pulling off long-term goals. Self-control and some level of sacrifice are often needed to achieve greater rewards down the line— a point that elite athletes like Serena and Venus Williams understand very well. Nonetheless, the lure of short-term thrills can overcome even high-functioning, disciplined professionals. I recall an article about a young doctor found dead in the lobby of an apartment building. She'd overdosed on drugs before apparently being abandoned by someone she thought was a friend. This woman must have exercised quite a bit of discipline and delayed gratification to make it through medical school and residency training, and yet somehow she'd lost her way.

IF NOT FINANCIAL SUCCESS, THEN WHAT?

We may understand that we need a bigger source of motivation beyond instant gratification through material gain, but it's not always easy to know what that is. For example, some years back my job gave me the opportunity to relocate myself and my family to Sydney, Australia. That made sense to me for a number of reasons. Beyond the professional opportunities it would provide me, I wanted to give my kids the experience of living in an environment that could help them develop a global mindset—or at least reduce their stress through more relaxed academic standards compared with those in Singapore's education system.

I also saw a chance to spend more time with my family. If I were based in Australia, I could do my work without having to be away from home as often. Instead of weeklong international trips throughout Asia, I'd just travel a day or two here and there among a few major Australian cities. Better career options, more time with family, less academic pressure on the kids—all things considered, relocating to Australia seemed like the obvious choice: that is, until my now ex-wife voiced her doubts.

"What will the kids and I do in a place where we don't know anyone, especially while you're away on trips?" she asked. That question led me to think about how much my kids would miss growing up with their cousins and spending time with their aunts, uncles, and grandparents.

She was absolutely right. While trying to give my son and daughter a "better childhood," I overlooked their emotional need for familial and social support networks. I thought of the joy E and S got from weekly visits with extended family: the love and support of being around aunts, uncles, and grandparents; the hugs and squeals of excitement on seeing their cousins; the endless laughter as they chased each other around or curled up together on the couch to play games.

I already knew how important my kids' happiness was to me, but I'd been thinking about it all wrong. Once I realized the deeper value at play was connection to family and community, the decision to remain in Singapore became easier.

When first considering a move to Sydney, I looked mainly at material benefits—my career and the kids' education, which could boost their later career success—at the expense of broader family and community support. I've been duped more than once by this fallacy, thinking that a successful career (and demonstrating my wealth through fancy possessions) and a less challenging path for the kids' education (which would lead to better grades, a path to an elite university, etc.) would somehow guarantee a happier, more fulfilling life.

In his book *The Happiness Advantage*, author and happiness researcher Shawn Achor challenges the tendency to associate happiness with achievement. This conditioning often starts in primary school and continues through high school, where we're told to aim for the highest grades and earn top scores on university entrance exams. Next we chase college degrees, more test scores, more advanced degrees. Once we enter the workforce, we endlessly pursue the next promotion, the fancier title, the bigger office, or the higher salary.

When functioning this way, we almost ensure we're never satisfied, because there's always some goal we haven't achieved.

Achor argues that the logic works better in reverse—that success follows happiness rather than the other way around. So . . . what do we make of the marshmallow experiment? Perhaps the answer is simply that kids who already feel more secure and happy find it easier to delay gratification, having less need for some immediate external reward.

Of course, the larger issue is that the marshmallow studies measured traditional, achievement-based markers of success such as academic performance and income levels—rather than corresponding reports on actual *happiness*. Even if you can control yourself, delay gratification, and achieve "success," you're not guaranteed happiness. After all, I achieved a career a kid like me should have had little chance of doing. Yet, even after attaining money and status, I felt miserable.

Perhaps the payout needs to be more meaningful than money or status, greater than some "bigger payout" of the same dopamine source—*more* money, *more* status, multiple marshmallows versus just one. It seems that we can't just develop willpower and success and—poof!—attain lasting happiness.

So let's turn back to Aristotle.

Aristotle believed that all people seek happiness, which (like it or not) is best achieved through living a virtuous life—that is, by contemplating and pursuing the highest virtue.

To me, a virtuous life is to find and live our life's meaning and purpose—a decidedly more Aristotelian view (at least as I interpret it). With that higher meaning and purpose in mind, we can lay out a road map to guide our decisions toward the final destination. This allows us to see whether each action brings us closer to the path aligned with our meaning and purpose—or down a tempting detour that leads to regret.

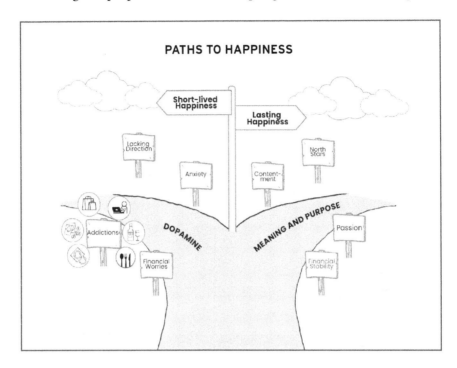

So what do we do with all of this? I interpret it to mean that achieving true happiness takes more than simply delaying gratification and achieving success. It means living in accordance with our own deeper meaning and purpose. And since humans are complex, we each need to figure out for ourselves what that highest virtue looks like for us personally.

If you had asked me to define happiness as a high school graduate in the 1980s, I would've had no clue. I certainly would not have associated it with some higher virtue. Beyond looking cool, having fun, and impressing girls, I didn't give the matter much thought.

Even after achieving financial success through exercising delayed gratification and developing a high degree of self-discipline, I was still no closer to finding any semblance of lasting happiness. Indeed, for many of us, happiness seems as hard to find as it is to define. Instead of continuing on the hedonic treadmill from my youth and early adult life, it finally dawned on me that the path to lasting happiness comes down to finding and living my meaning and purpose.

TAKEAWAYS

Looking back in history, we find great thinkers debating the nature of happiness. From ancient Nordics through the Middle Ages and Renaissance, the concept of "happiness" was likely defined as lucky happenstance or even luxury—until forces like industrialization and American political theory brought the "pursuit of happiness" front and center for the masses. Shifting work and consumer trends during and since the Enlightenment have caused many to conflate happiness with material goods and passing pleasures, evoking ancient Greek philosopher Aristippus's *hedonic* definition of happiness.

But for an immoderate, pleasure-chasing kid like me, Aristippus's approach was never going to yield long-term happiness—and I'm not alone. Modern behavioral studies and neuroscience show that acknowledging our impulses and insecurities, then learning self-discipline, can help us work toward more substantive, sustainable results. By exercising restraint, we can forgo short-term gains and achieve long-term success.

Still, that's only part of the equation. Many individuals—myself included—achieve real professional and financial success in our careers only to find ourselves feeling lost. Enter Aristotle. This famous philosopher's musings help us identify both the "what" (happiness) and the "how" (living a virtuous life) of human existence. In short, Aristotle recommended a life of self-reflection and living in accordance with our own personal "highest virtue." Or, as I define it, living our life's meaning and purpose.

Even for those of us who've achieved professional and financial success, finding meaning and purpose is not always a foregone conclusion. But, especially for those of us who grew up either poor and struggling or those of us lacking discipline and direction, the "virtuous life" can sound like a drag, especially when there's instant gratification on hand. What we need next is the "why." As the German philosopher Friedrich Nietzsche so deftly put it, "He who has a 'why' to live for can bear almost any 'how.'"[2]

Let's now walk through the first step of this journey—how to locate the unique "highest virtue" that determines your "why." Your unique source of lasting, eudaimonic happiness—a kind of personal North Star by which to establish a road map for this journey of life.

LEARNING POINTS

- The active pursuit of happiness is a relatively modern phenomenon in the context of human history.

- You can choose to pursue *short-lived happiness* (pleasure seeking) or *lasting happiness* (living our meaning and purpose).

- Career and financial success may still leave you feeling unfulfilled, as though your life lacks something greater.

- To stay true to your path to lasting happiness, you need to find your "why."

SELF-REFLECTION

- Are your actions more aligned with chasing the next dopamine hit or searching for life's meaning and purpose?

- Do you find it difficult to stay the course in pursuing lasting happiness, and if so, why?

2

FINDING YOUR NORTH STAR

Finding your North Star helps you live with purpose, and it gives you a reference point to keep you moving in the right direction.

—Paula Black[1]

The year 2000 found me in Hong Kong with a lucrative career, a drawerful of designer watches, and a deep, pervading inner emptiness. As I began questioning why success left me feeling hollow, a former boss got in touch with a job opportunity. She was returning to Singapore to build a subsidiary for one of the world's most successful investment firms, and she wanted me to help grow the new enterprise.

I felt torn. On one hand, I held her in high esteem and knew she would create a positive, dynamic work environment. However, the opportunity came with a cost: a huge reduction in pay and corporate standing. This offer marked one of the first moments I thought to ask myself what would *truly* make me happy. Without knowing it, I'd begun a kind of philosophical quest for meaning.

As it happened, my first answers came not from a philosopher or religious guru meditating on some hilltop—but instead from an aging general practitioner I'd met in Singapore. I trusted and respected this man, and I had an inkling he might shed light on my problem. To be honest, I barely even knew the guy. Still, something about him felt wise, even paternal—which, considering that my own father passed away when I was in my early twenties, may explain why I sought his advice.

So I composed an email to this friendly near-stranger, outlining my conundrum: I'd grown unhappy in my job. Still, I wasn't sure about the pay cut attached to my new offer. I even threw in the option of returning to school to earn that degree in psychology I'd initially pursued in college—before the prospect of earning more money drove me to change my major to finance. I provided this man a long, unsolicited, and comprehensive analysis for each option and hit Send—not knowing if I'd ever hear back.

Miraculously, he responded. In contrast to my long-winded message, his was both brief and profound. As I recall, he wrote: "You're looking for happiness in the wrong place. For most, happiness comes from Serving God, Serving Society, or Serving Family. Once you find your source of happiness, you will realize that your job is nothing more than a means to that end."

In short, the good doctor believed that to know lasting happiness, we must first find our highest personal motivating virtue: the true guiding light that never sets (though other forces may dim or even obscure it at times).

It would take me a little while to make sense of this advice. Before I could find that source of happiness aligning my path with my core values and leading the way to a more meaningful, lasting form of happiness, I had to figure out what my core values even were.

WHAT BRINGS US HAPPINESS?

Several years after joining my ex-boss in Singapore, I still struggled to find any semblance of happiness despite sacrificing pay, career progression, and passion in my life. So, I revisited that physician's claims. Could he be right about the sources of lasting happiness? More research, I decided, was in order.

The first thing I noticed was that, while there's copious material to be found—from scholarly reports to philosophical treatises to YouTube videos—on the *definitions* (e.g., hedonic vs. eudaimonistic) and *mechanisms* of happiness (e.g., exercising self-restraint and delayed gratification), considerably less can be found on *concrete sources* of happiness.

What did I find instead? Lots of advice about mindset and lifestyle choices: Find work you're passionate about, cultivate healthy habits, practice mindfulness. I found a lot related to generosity and—especially—*gratitude*. After a while, though, I noticed two main themes. The first was the connection between strong personal relationships and happiness.

The Harvard Medical School has backed up the link between happiness and meaningful human connection. In 2017, they published findings on a 75-plus-year study to identify predictors of healthy aging by tracking the mental and physical health, career enjoyment, marital quality, and retirement experience of 268 Harvard–educated men.[2] Simultaneous to Harvard's study, a parallel effort called the Glueck Study (also out of Harvard) tracked the same predictors among 456 disadvantaged, inner-city Boston men. Both studies reported that the strength and warmth of interpersonal relationships throughout life impact overall satisfaction more than anything else. In fact, Harvard found that strong relationships predict good health outcomes better than cholesterol levels.

The second echoed Aristotle's thought, namely that meaning and purpose—rather than money and pleasure—generate the most lasting happiness. Speaking of our friend, Aristotle, let's briefly unpack his concept of *eudaimonia*. He broke the term into four levels: fleeting happiness derived from material objects (*laetus*) and ego gratification (*felix*)—plus the deeper well-being that comes from doing good for others (*beautitudo*). In other words, he acknowledged that while there's fleeting happiness to be found in serving yourself, the kind that lasts comes from serving others. But that's not all. Aristotle also believed the highest, most transcendent form of happiness (*sublime beautitudo*) comes from achieving a balance of those three levels, as well as "finding your own calling."

More recently, Martin Seligman, the pioneer of positive psychology, categorized levels of happiness, from "the pleasant life" filled with positive emotions to "the good life," which involves employing virtues and strengths to enhance our own lives. For Seligman, "the meaningful life"—achieved when utilizing our virtues and strengths for a "purpose greater than ourselves"—tops the list.[3]

Beyond balancing levels of happiness, what do we make of that *second* part of Aristotle's most "sublime" version of happiness—namely, the idea of "finding your own calling"?

Could that have something to do with what Nietzsche meant when he talked about a "why" to help bear "almost any 'how'"?

While the categories of Serving Family, Society, and/or God don't explicitly appear in these thinkers' work, the doctor I'd confided in placed a central focus on *service*, which echoes through notions of human connectivity, altruism, and living according to virtues and values.

In the end, I began to suspect that the doctor's advice just might hold up. If building strong relationships and acting according to our values bring happiness, maybe the concept of service—whether to family, society, and/or God—can help lead the way to finding our core motivator. But how do we, as individuals, decide which of these three sources of happiness represent our own true calling? How do we find that constant, guiding light to set our personal course?

PASSING ON OUR EMOTIONAL BAGGAGE

After my career move to Singapore failed to bring any semblance of fulfillment, I took a closer look at the doctor's response—and why it hadn't resonated with me before. I wasn't opposed to his input; in fact, it made a lot of sense to me. The simplicity of his advice appealed to my pragmatic side. If we could whittle down all possible sources of lasting happiness to just three options, how hard could it be for me to pick the right one?

The first—Serving God—felt relatively easy to dismiss. Although a Lutheran church sponsored my family's immigration to the US, religion never featured meaningfully within my formative years. Dad was a self-proclaimed atheist, and I'd describe my mother as a ritualistic Buddhist, in contrast to a more philosophical or overtly spiritual expression of the faith.

Serving Society seemed a feasible option for me. I've always been involved in social work, in one form or another, since beginning my career. But even though I love giving back, deep down I knew it wasn't my central calling in life. Reflecting on what I'd be willing to sacrifice without payback, I couldn't honestly say that Serving Society had been a strong enough reason to effectively direct my internal compass.

That left me with Serving Family. But that also didn't feel right, largely because I was single at the time. Beyond that, if I had to honestly choose which sustained me more, my family or friends, I would have answered—without any hesitation—friends. A lot of it came down to my childhood of benign neglect, since both my parents worked long hours in Cambodia—my father as the general manager of a small commercial airline and my mother running her own small printing business out of the first floor of our rented home.

Beyond that, my earliest recollections of familial love and attention mainly centered on my paternal grandfather in Cambodia. A family helper also tended to my early years, but my greatest joy came from morning strolls with my grandfather through the parks and streets of my birth country. Sadly, my time with him was short-lived, as he suddenly left Cambodia soon after the civil war began—when I was just five years old.

After arriving in Portland, Oregon, my parents focused almost solely on surviving in this new, unfamiliar country. As a result, I learned not to depend on anyone in my family for emotional support. Taking my family history into account, I'm not surprised that the concept of Serving Family failed for so long to resonate with me as a possible source of happiness.

Like many American youth, my siblings and I all moved away to college and then to wherever our jobs led us. I started to think that maybe my personal disconnect from family, society, and religion had somehow thrown off my natural internal compass, interrupted by the artificial magnetism of hedonic pleasures, status, success, and "rugged individualism"—that is, by focusing on self above other people and higher virtues.

MY ANGELINA JOLIE MOMENT

It would take a serendipitous encounter before I could comprehend the full weight of the doctor's advice and locate my personal source of lasting happiness.

By then, I was in my early forties and still single. Relationship after relationship seemed to fizzle out. A concerned friend noticed how I struggled to form healthy romantic relationships and gifted me a book on the topic, titled *Love Is a Choice*. Written by three mental health professionals, the book examines the roots and mechanisms of codependency and recommends steps to establish healthier relationship patterns in adulthood.

The authors emphasize the need for children to receive love from parents. In their words, this love fills the child's "love tank." This provides a sense of emotional completeness, empowering the child to move on to establish healthy romantic adult relationships.

As I read the book, it felt as though the authors were describing me.

But what could I do about it? I was already an adult, and I couldn't go back in time. Even if I could, I still wouldn't have been able to change how my parents and caretakers operated.

One day, I found myself sitting in a neurologist's office talking about my difficulties sleeping. Somehow, we got on the subject of people we admire. The neurologist said she most admired Angelina Jolie.

Angelina Jolie? I thought, incredulous and amused. Here's an accomplished scientist pointing to a controversial movie star as some shining example of humankind.

Perhaps if she had said Meryl Streep, I would have accepted her response at face value and moved on from the conversation—and I may still be brooding over the mystery of lasting happiness today.

Instead, on seeing my surprised look, the neurologist explained. What she admired about Jolie wasn't her beauty or acting success, but rather her service to others. Jolie had been appointed as special envoy for the United Nations High Commissioner for Refugees agency, in addition to her work as a mother committed to raising a healthy family.

"Generous, dedicated, successful," said the neurologist, before adding with a laugh, "Plus, she is dating Brad Pitt! What more do you want?"

Growing up in America, I'd thought of Jolie as a divorcee in her twenties and overall lost soul, best known at the time for nailing the film role of a young psychopath and wearing a vial of Billy Bob Thornton's blood around her neck. In a 2021 interview with the *Guardian*, she described her teenage years as overwhelmingly empty and discussed her attempts to fill the void through drugs, alcohol, and self-harm.[4]

Then it struck me. *Perhaps,* I thought, *Jolie struggled until she found her source of lasting happiness in a family of her own.* After all, everything seemed to change after she adopted her first child, Maddox (who also happens to hail from Cambodia).

What if it's possible to fill the void left over by an early lack of unconditional love—by giving the same to our children? If Angelina Jolie could do that, maybe I could too. That was when I began revisiting the idea that family—my very own—could become a source of lasting happiness for me. For so long, I'd poured all my energy into my career, but it just hadn't filled the void. Maybe Lee Iacocca, CEO and chairman of Chrysler, wasn't exaggerating when he said, "I've had a wonderful and successful career. But next to my family, it really hasn't mattered at all."

Long story short, no more than a few years after my fateful visit to the neurologist, I was married and awaiting our first child. E's birth immediately confirmed my hopeful revelation in that neurologist's office. I remember standing in the hospital delivery room, looking at my newborn son with tears of joy, finally understanding what unconditional love felt like. Beyond that, I felt a new and profound sense of groundedness. For the first time in my life, the emptiness I'd been carrying around filled with a happiness rooted in meaning—finally something to guide my life's journey.

It seemed like the clouds parted to reveal my true source of joy. Becoming a father clarified my "why" and sharpened my focus. I now felt I could make decisions more confidently—through the lens of ensuring the best possible future for my children. I knew, for example, I wouldn't so readily take a huge pay cut to chase greater personal fulfillment through work as an end unto itself.

However, by instinctively leaning into my provider role, I admittedly lost balance and leaned too far. I worked longer hours and spent more and more time away from my family as my role involved inordinate travel across numerous time zones.

During the COVID-19 pandemic, I looked up and realized that working this much to support my family actually kept me away from what matters most. In fact, my marriage was falling apart and I'd already missed out on so much of my children's growing-up years.

I questioned whether I was really Serving Family.

Before we go on, I need to clarify that having kids to fill a void of unconditional love was *not* what the authors of *Love Is a Choice* prescribed for filling depleted "love tanks" and healing adult codependency. It's not what I'm saying either. Simply having children will not automatically heal past wounds and fill your life with meaning and purpose.

I only share this story because it served as a wake-up call and catalyst to help *me* understand the importance of family as an underlying guiding light, even for someone who once seemed hopelessly adrift. It would be grossly irresponsible of me to suggest that having children can solve all your problems and magically fix dysfunctional patterns.

While, for me, having children marked the first step toward filling the emptiness within me, I still needed to continue examining and aligning my actions with my priorities.

OUR SOURCE(S) OF LASTING HAPPINESS

So, how do you find your own source(s) of lasting happiness?

Answering this question can take a bit of time and a lot of self-examination. Unfortunately, it's not as easy as picking up a compass and following the direction indicated on the dial—nor is it nearly as romantic as stargazing from the helm of a ship.

It's not uncommon for people not to figure out their true grounding until well into adulthood (if ever). It may even feel like your source of happiness shifts, for example, after retirement or upon welcoming a baby into your family. However, I believe that, for the vast majority of people, our source stays the same—though other influences in life may temporarily cloud it from view. I also believe that Serving Family represents the source most likely to bring lasting happiness to most people. This may sound bold, even presumptuous, but let me explain.

I agree with the good doctor that other sources, including Serving God and Serving Society, do shine brighter for some. However, I suspect they're in the minority. I'm not talking about teaching Sunday school once a week or volunteering at a homeless shelter once a month. As I see it, Serving God or Serving Society only qualify as one's true source of happiness if they make this service the central, leading force in their life—surpassing and/or directing all other considerations. I'm talking about people who renounce career opportunities and/or "normal" family life to join the clergy or monastic life, or who devote their lives entirely to social causes. Think Nelson Mandela, who, despite having a family, gave up his personal freedom and spent 27 years in jail to stand for social justice in South Africa. Such people sacrifice any amount of money or time with family because they feel certain of their higher calling.

After recognizing my own failure to balance time between work and family, I realized I needed to account for those times when I might lose my sense of direction in life. Think of the workaholic dad I had become. Or the televangelist ostensibly "Serving God"—while begging strangers for donations and living in a multimillion-dollar home with a private jet. Other times, personal pursuits and ambitions distract us from our true priority.

In light of this, I added a fourth source: Serving Self. This suggests there may be people who truly derive more lifelong happiness from serving themselves than by Serving Family, Society, or God. Although I suppose that might be true, I firmly believe that, for the vast majority of people, this way of life eventually leads to an inner emptiness and isolation similar to what I experienced when chasing material gains, personal enjoyment, and achievement alone. We can all think of greedy or corrupt politicians or business leaders who seem to only live for their own benefit, though I doubt whether such people can be truly described as happy.

This doesn't mean we should martyr ourselves in service to others. It should go without saying that there is a healthy, balanced way to serve the self, including maintaining a healthy body and mind and developing our interests. That said, I believe most of us attain more lasting happiness when contributing to something bigger than ourselves—even if some of us take a while to figure that out.

Although the doctor I confided in suggested we each have just one source of lasting happiness, I began to question this logic. Many friends and family members struggled to choose just one—instead citing two or even three sources. I realized that while most people feel *more* pulled by one, a second source tends to also influence the course of their lives.

Why stop at two and not three main sources of lasting happiness? I've noticed, in particular, my friends most committed to a religious faith often claim all three main sources of lasting happiness: Serving God, Serving Family, and Serving Society. However, keep in mind the motivation behind our actions, not to whom we direct them. I argue that, for most people of faith, their social work derives from Serving God. In other words, unless you're a monk who spends days and nights praying in solitude, you're likely serving *people* in your community as a consequence of your service to God. For such individuals, I'd name Serving Family and Serving God as their two main sources of lasting happiness (as opposed to those who devote much or most of their lives to community service without being led by faith or spirituality).

As I wrote this book, I discovered that Polaris, the Earth's North Star is actually a star system composed of three stars. Interestingly enough, one star, Polaris A, vastly outshines the others, followed by Polaris Ab. The third, Polaris B, appears much dimmer and farther away from these other two. While my conclusions preceded my discovery of the Polaris system, I was pleased to see how well the metaphor holds up.

FINDING OUR NORTH STAR

I'm not the first to write about the concept of a personal North Star, and I'm sure I won't be the last. From what I've read, it seems that some define the personal North Star as our "passion." As you might guess by the title of this book, I do believe passion plays a significant role in our finding meaning and purpose—as I'll develop in later chapters. However, I define the personal North Star differently. Instead of one North Star, I believe that most of us have two—a primary Polaris A and a secondary Polaris Ab. In discovering our primary North Star, our Polaris A, we take the first step toward finding meaning. While our primary North Star shines brighter and takes center stage, our secondary

North Star, our Polaris Ab, helps direct our purpose. Our North Star constellation helps us create meaning and build purpose by reminding us of the "why" that helps us endure any "how" (as Nietzsche put it).

By now, you may be pondering the two main sources of lasting happiness for yourself—assuming that you have more than one. But how do you uncover the one *main* North Star to guide your primary path? Let's take my former colleague Alex, for example. He was quick to point to both Serving Society and Serving Family—in that order of priority. After all, he chose to work in human resources, specializing in learning and development, because he wanted to give back to society. When negotiating his last employment contract during the time we worked together, Alex focused more on his love for his purpose-driven work, with only a secondary consideration to pay.

When I asked about his family, I learned he was married, but he and his wife at the time didn't have any children. Next, I posed the following scenario: *The Peace Corps asks you to commit two years of your life to living in Micronesia to set up a training program for people in need. They'll provide for daily living expenses, but you'll need to leave your wife behind to pay the mortgage and other living expenses in Singapore during this mission.*

After pausing a moment, Alex quickly retracted his earlier answer. Facing this consequential—if hypothetical—question forces a singular choice, which tends to put things into perspective. This doesn't mean that Alex isn't motivated by Serving Society, but it does suggest that his higher priority (and, therefore, his main North Star) is Serving Family.

Another example is my friend Eleanor who works in the insurance industry. Although she's a working mother of two children, religion features so prominently in her life that she insisted on Serving God as her primary North Star, followed by Serving Family. During one of our talks, I tested her conviction with the following scenario: *Your children have grown and started families of their own. As a retired couple, you and your husband decide to go on a two-year mission to Cambodia to spread the Lord's Gospel. In the first six months you receive a phone call from your son back in Singapore. He informs you that he and his wife desperately need support with their children. He asks you to consider coming home to Singapore to help.*

I fully expected Eleanor to backpedal like Alex had done—but to my surprise, she stayed the course. The first thing she said she would do was to pray to God for an answer.

"What if God directs you to continue your mission?" I asked.

"Then God must have a plan for our son," she said, firmly. "It's not my place to doubt God's plan and get in the way of what my son is meant to learn from his personal plight." I have no doubt that, based on this response, Eleanor's main North Star truly is Serving God, followed by a Polaris Ab of Serving Family.

A number of people I've spoken to feel that the order of our primary and secondary North Stars change as we transition from one stage of life to another. For example, one of my retired friends, Greg, recently told me that his priority shifted from Serving Family to Serving Society after his children left Singapore to start their respective careers in the US and the UK. Nowadays, Greg spends a lot more time working with his favorite charity. As you might have guessed, I asked what he would do if one of his children urgently needed his support. *Would you drop your charity work to help?* Greg's swift, confident "yes" revealed his true guiding principle of Serving Family had not changed.

As you can see, considering a hypothetical choice between your top two sources of lasting happiness can help clarify your dominant North Star. I believe this also holds true for young people who have yet to start families of their own. When looking for early feedback on this book, I spoke to Elliott, then a 19-year-old university student who struggled to choose between Serving Society and Serving Family. When asked to consider what he would do if his mother fell seriously ill and needed his help, he quickly realized where his priorities lay. Elliott wouldn't think twice about putting his social work activities (including school) on hold to be with his mom in her time of need. When Elliott becomes a parent himself, I have no doubt that he would do the same for his children.

Just like the Earth's faithful Polaris A, I believe that, with very few exceptions, every person's true North Star remains unchanged throughout their life. Granted, our clarity of vision may vary, causing the sky to temporarily cloud over its guiding light. In addition, the amount of time or money we spend on each source of lasting happiness may change as we move from one phase of life to another. But when faced with a stark life choice (like those hypotheticals posed to Alex, Eleanor, Greg, and Elliott), our priorities will reveal themselves. Similarly, when Eugene O'Kelly, author of *Chasing Daylight*, faced his terminal diagnosis, he quickly and profoundly understood the importance of his true North. Hopefully, the rest of us can be more proactive about finding our primary North Star—without costly mistakes, high-stakes choices, or imminent tragedy forcing our hands.

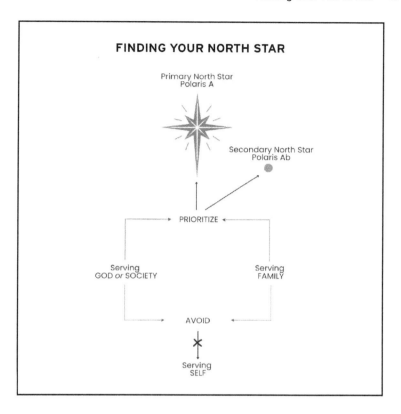

I admit that my definitions of our primary and secondary North Stars sound perhaps overly simplistic. However, rather than debating semantics, I urge you to consider whether these ideas make sense, and, more importantly, could guide your life toward lasting happiness. Serving Family truly helps me wake up every day and forge ahead despite challenges that can seem insurmountable. It also simplifies matters when I have a major decision to make—a job offer, investment opportunity, or even new hobby—I simply ask myself whether each choice will move me closer to or further away from my main source of lasting happiness. I find that, since locking in my primary North Star, the rest of my priorities (including my Polaris Ab) tend to fall into place.

Looking back, I now see that the email from that physician offered sage advice. However, at the time—and for years afterward—it didn't resonate. I remained convinced that I would indeed find happiness working with a company and leader whose values seemed to match my own.

As you may have guessed, that wasn't the case. My inner emptiness persisted, exacerbated by a major management reshuffle six years in, which left me again looking for a change. It took several more years and experiencing parenthood before I understood what prevented my happiness—and came to see just how right both Aristotle and that old doctor had been.

TAKEAWAYS

When it comes to finding our respective sources of lasting happiness, there are no right or wrong answers. This is an exercise in self-exploration, not some pop quiz. The idea is to understand who we are and what motivates us at our core be it through service to family, society, or God. Admittedly, the whole thing can get quite confusing, especially if you've experienced traumas related to family, faith, or where you fit into society.

To complicate matters further, many (though not all) of us can locate more than one guiding light (much like the Polaris star system). For those with two competing sources, Polaris A is the one dearest to our hearts—and this never changes over time. It's the route we would take when those paths dramatically split and we have to pick just one. It's the one we'd never dream of sacrificing, the reason we get up every morning. This dominant North Star provides the strength to face periods of extreme challenges and make it to the other side.

Aside from our primary North Star, our Polaris Ab (second source of lasting happiness) will also play a role in finding meaning and purpose, as we'll explore later in this book.

A true primary North Star (Polaris A) doesn't shift or change as we move from one stage of life to another. Nor is it necessarily determined by the amount of time or money that we spend on each source of happiness at any given time.

Finding our North Stars is only the first step to finding and fostering meaning and purpose. And, if we're being honest, most of us won't go the route of Mother Teresa or Nelson Mandela and renounce all material gains or personal freedoms to follow a primary North Star of Serving God or Serving Society. In fact (especially if I'm right that most of us can find our guiding light in family), the hard truth is that we need to balance and support this source of happiness with earning a living. While meaning, purpose, and passion may be life's greatest portions, we also need some way of supporting it all. Put bluntly, we need money too.

After understanding the importance of *lasting* happiness over short-lived enjoyment, and finding our main and secondary sources of lasting happiness (Polaris A and Polaris Ab, respectively), the next chapter will ground us back into the practicalities of life.

The next step toward creating a meaningful, purpose-driven life (and eventually closing the Passion Gap) has to do with, yes, money. Specifically, both in terms of understanding our relationship with money in the context of serving our North Stars, and in figuring out how much will bring us happiness/contentment. In other words, how much money is enough?

LEARNING POINTS

- True lasting happiness typically comes not from self-gratification but through service to family, society, or faith.

- You may have more than one source of lasting happiness, but the one that you prioritize over the other is your primary *North Star*—the "why" that helps you "bear almost any 'how.'"

- How you choose to use your time and resources may change through the different phases of your life, but your North Star priorities remain the same.

- Finding your North Stars—your Polaris A and Polaris Ab—is the first step in your journey to finding your life's meaning and purpose.

SELF-REFLECTION

- What are your two sources of lasting happiness?

- Which one is your true North Star (Polaris A)?

3

MONEY AND HAPPINESS— HOW MUCH IS ENOUGH?

Too many people spend money they earned to buy things they don't want to impress people that they don't like.

—Will Rogers

A few years ago, while strolling through a nearby mall with his mom and sister, my son, E, turned a corner to find several gleaming BMWs on display. Like many nine-year-old boys, E loves cars. On seeing E's excitement, one of the salespeople waved him over and helped him inside a sleek convertible BMW 6 Series.

Knowing E, I can imagine the look in his eyes—it was love at first sight. He may not have been able to drive, but he knew he was sitting in a beautiful car whose cool factor was off the charts. What he didn't know was that the starting sticker price of that vehicle far exceeds the annual salary of most Americans and, in this case, most Singaporeans. In a 2023 article, the BBC cited Singapore as *the* most expensive country in the world in which to own a car.[1]

Parked in our driveway at home was (and still remains) a low-end European-made sedan. Compared to the brand-new BMW 6 Series, my 2015 Mercedes c180 retails at less than half the price (and a mere fraction of the coolness). Later, as E breathlessly described his dream ride to me, my inner nine-year-old delighted in his vision of cruising down the highway with the top down. I also remembered my high school shame about my dad's station wagon, which to my teen mind had to be the most embarrassingly cliched family vehicle ever made.

That day with E, I sensed an opportunity—not only to justify my boring automotive tastes to my impressionable son, but also to impart a broader life lesson. I explained that while I could afford to buy a much nicer car (like his beloved BMW 6 Series), doing so didn't fit within my value system. For me, it's far more important to own a reliable car that keeps him and his sister safe, while ensuring financial security for our family. As far as I'm concerned, a car is just a piece of metal that gets us from point A to point B. So long as it does so dependably and safely, it's right for me.

What I wanted to pass on to E that day was that (for better or worse) we all develop a system of values that dictates how we make decisions, including financial ones. We each aspire to provide a certain lifestyle for ourselves and those we love. For example, I've prioritized owning a car in a country with prohibitively high associated costs (not to mention the torrential rain and smothering humidity) because I value the convenience and comfort of driving my two children to and from their schools and numerous after school activities instead of using public transportation. That said, there's a point where my values meet—and limit—my aspirations, and that point happens to look like a low-end European sedan.

To make the right choices in life, we need to know what's most important to us, which starts with recognizing our North Stars, those main guiding lights for lasting happiness. That said, life is not some philosophical theory; it's a practical exercise in managing expectations and navigating uncertainties—all of which (let's face it) requires money.

So how do finances factor into the happiness equation, not simply in relation to shiny cars and collectible watches, but as foundational support for that all-important set of North Stars?

I decided to investigate and learn how income impacts happiness, not only from researchers who study this subject but also from those who seem to have both aspects of life pretty well figured out, including Warren Buffett, a billionaire business magnate famous for his modest lifestyle and well-grounded family values.

MEASURING UP

When examining the relationship between money and happiness, researchers seem to take two broadly different approaches. The first approach involves comparison, specifically: how comparing our finances to those of others impacts our happiness.

We've all heard the phrase "keeping up with the Joneses." It was coined in 1913 by Arthur R. "Pop" Momand, whose comic strip (the original *Keeping Up with the Joneses*) joked about his society's rampant consumerism. Momand's comic strip was inspired by the earlier work of American sociologist Thorstein Veblen, who observed how the nouveau riche showed off their newly acquired status by introducing another now familiar phrase: "conspicuous consumption."

In 2009, Pennsylvania State University sociologist Glenn Firebaugh led a study into how different relative income levels among peer groups affect the happiness of Americans across different age groups.[2] He found participants reported feeling happier when living in richer neighborhoods compared to poorer ones, even when neighbors in their nicer part of town outearned them. However, the happiest respondents tended to be people living in a bubble of relative wealth within the context of an overall poorer county. In other words, wealth does seem to bring more happiness when the wealthy live near—but not *too* near—relative poverty.

Other scholars of the income-happiness question, including social psychologist Edward Diener (nicknamed Dr. Happiness), co-authored a study published in 2002 that found those living in wealthier countries are generally happier. However, the study warned against pursuing material possessions over other values for such individuals. The authors concluded with the following: "our advice is to avoid poverty, live in a rich country, and focus on goals other than material wealth."[3]

Most of us understand that trying to keep up with the Joneses quickly becomes a losing game. There will always be someone with a larger bank account, newer car, or more expensive toy. Such a hedonistic path rarely leads to happy endings. Instead, it locks us into that dopamine-seeking cycle of diminishing returns. Too often, we end up financially and emotionally distressed—much like the fictional McGinises of Momand's comic.

Today's world of social media and overall digital connectivity has upped the ante. Now we can compare ourselves not only to those we personally know and see every day, but also to millions of strangers bent on garnering as many clicks and subscribers as possible. Often, this means displaying their (real or perceived) wealth, triggering the desire in us to follow suit, whether we can afford to or not. Meanwhile, as companies and social media "influencers" push expensive products and services, it's getting harder to distinguish between what's *possible* and what's *probable* (or even desirable) for us personally. When we're trapped in such a mindset, no amount of wealth will suffice.

CLIMBING THE LADDER

The second camp of happiness scholars explored what happens to individuals' happiness when their income grows—sometimes arriving at somewhat contradictory conclusions. In 2010, Princeton University researchers Daniel Kahneman and Angus Deaton arrived at an approximate sum of money that correlated with optimal happiness among their sample population: US$75,000 per year. Above that, a "declining margin of utility" set in. In other words, happiness levels appeared to level off once incomes rose above US$75,000. Results of a 2018 Purdue University study even suggest that happiness levels begin *declining* upon reaching US$105,000.[4] One possible reason is we start down that old path of keeping up with the Joneses.

Fast-forward to 2021, when a study conducted by Matthew Killingsworth, a senior fellow at the Wharton School of Business, found that despite these studies, there may not be any income-related happiness plateau (or descent) after all. Killingsworth and his team instead saw happiness levels continue to rise as incomes increased. As he explained to *Penn Today*, Killingsworth believed this has to do with the increased sense of control over one's life that money brings: "Across decisions big and small, having more money gives a person more choices and a greater sense of autonomy."[5]

To put the discrepancies found in their respective conclusions to rest, Killingsworth and Princeton's Kahneman collaborated on a follow-up study. In 2023, they found that, when taking "happiness *disposition*" into account, those previously observed income-related happiness plateaus can be explained. Their joint research uncovered such a plateau only among the unhappiest 20 percent of the population, and only once their income levels reached US$100,000.[6] According to Killingsworth, greater incomes still equate to increased happiness for most of us, with the notable exception of "people who are financially well-off but unhappy."

"If you're rich and miserable," Killingsworth said, "more money won't help."

Outside of people somehow "disposed" toward misery, the co-researchers found that higher incomes continued to result in higher reported states of well-being, with no discernable cap. In fact, among the happiest 30 percent, levels of happiness *accelerated* as their incomes increased beyond US$100,000. (They drew no conclusions for those earning more than US$500,000 due to a lack of data points.)

I'm no academic, but the conclusion of the joint Killingsworth–Kahneman study—especially this idea of "the more the merrier" for those who are not disposed to being unhappy—fails to resonate with me.

How do we reconcile these apparently conflicting messages and decide for ourselves how much money is enough to support a contented, happy life? To me, it's not comparing ourselves to others or how much we earn. Rather it's figuring out how much is enough for each of us—then learning to avoid the trappings of lifestyle creep.

WARREN BUFFETT AND LUNCH AT MCDONALD'S

Especially as a parent, I believe that our financial goals should align with our personal aspirations and values, especially those related to our North Stars.

To test this idea, I began looking for people who seem to grow their finances responsibly while leading genuinely happy lives. Luckily, I had no problem finding examples among friends and acquaintances who fit this bill. When I look at what these people share in common, I can see that whether Serving Family, Serving Society, or Serving God, these individuals know exactly what motivates them to get out of bed each morning, and they align their actions to those priorities—including those actions related to money.

I further noticed that, when talking to these people, two topics often came to the fore. The first was the importance of finding life partners who either share big-picture values (i.e. North Star priorities), as well as financial values—or who at least know how to compromise. Having personally experienced a painful divorce for these reasons, I couldn't agree more and won't add on to this topic as it is outside the scope of this chapter and book.

The second recurrent topic, interestingly enough, was the business magnate Warren Buffett. This multibillionaire and highly respected CEO of Berkshire Hathaway is as famous for the massive wealth he's acquired through uncanny investing skills as for his relatively modest lifestyle. Buffett still lives in an Omaha, Nebraska, home he bought in 1958 for a mere US$31,500, well before he became one of the world's richest men. While perhaps still a mansion by some people's standards (in 2023, Zillow.com estimates the inflation-adjusted value to be US$1.37 million[7]), this property currently reflects a value of less than .001 percent of Buffett's overall net worth of over $100 billion. He also drives the same (or similar) model Cadillac and eats at the same restaurants he did prior to amassing his billions of dollars—including McDonald's, where he once treated Bill Gates to lunch, paying while using coupons.[8]

In countless interviews, as well as a 2020 commencement speech at his alma mater, the University of Nebraska-Lincoln, Buffett emphasized the importance of relationships over that of money. In 2019, he told the *Financial Times*, "I can't buy time [and] I can't buy love."[9]

According to Buffett's daughter, his first priority has always been his family. In 2017, she explained to *People* magazine that despite his busy schedule, Buffett makes it a point to spend time with his numerous great-grandchildren, and he always knows what each of them is up to.

While he may represent an extreme example, Buffett's habits model how to avoid the dangers of lifestyle creep. Rather than inflating his spending each time his earnings rise, Buffett seems content to maintain his way of life, one rich in the emotional wealth that comes from aligning his actions with what matters most to him.

Behaving this way can protect all of us from the worst effects of income loss, whether from layoffs, failed business endeavors, and/or poor investments. The ability to live within our means—and recalibrate when needed—will help us to do what we love at work while earning enough to support our North Star values—which I call bridging our Passion Gap—in a faster and more sustainable way.

In other words, I believe that Buffett is unwaveringly clear on his true North Star: his family. Beyond that, I'm also convinced that, despite his being wealthy by anyone's standards, Buffett's relatively humble tastes and uncommon generosity suggest he's well-grounded when it comes to his Financial Baseline, as well as his Financial Aspirations and Financial Values (terms we'll define shortly).

FINDING EQUILIBRIUM

I've developed an approach to help me (and whoever else might find it useful) determine the income range needed to find and sustain long-term happiness. It involves three parts. First, your Financial Baseline, second, your Financial Aspirations, and finally, your Financial Values.

When I consider these three factors, the image of a hot-air balloon comes to mind. The first part, Financial Baseline, is the solid ground from which we launch. Think of this as the platform on which a hot-air balloon sits. For our purposes, the Financial Baseline gets determined largely (but not only) by the lifestyle in which we grew up.

The second component, Financial Aspirations, can be thought of as the gas we burn to lift off and navigate the skies. The stronger our Financial Aspirations, the higher our hot-air balloon wants to lift.

In this analogy, the last component, Financial Values, represents the sandbags that work to offset our ascent in a controlled, sustainable way. The point at which these opposing forces settle into airy equilibrium reveals our unique financial sweet spot: the lifestyle choice and related income level that, for us, promote long-term happiness.

Of course, our particular North Stars, and the intensity of our commitment to these guiding values, play a major role in influencing both our Financial Aspirations and our Financial Values. For example, when Serving Family, we might become more motivated to earn for our families. On the other hand, if our Polaris A is truly Serving God, we may have lower expectations for our lifestyle preferences and maintain stricter Financial Values.

Financial Baseline

I believe that for most of us, the lifestyle we experience in early childhood sets our basic expectations for what we "need" to feel materially secure—though we may aspire to something higher, or (less commonly) even lower than that. Note that I've used the term "lifestyle" rather than "income." This simplifies the approach a bit, since precise income levels don't lend themselves to an all-inclusive model for determining happiness. For one thing, the numbers can get out of control, considering the heights reached by some ultra-wealthy individuals. Plus, we'd need to make untold adjustments to account for variations in local economies and time periods, not to mention shifting inflation and other variables.

So, what do I mean by "lifestyle"? I like the definition provided by YourDictionary.com: "a style of living that reflects the attitudes and values of a person or group." This suggests that we each settle into lifestyle patterns and choices influenced by both personal values and aspirations—which tend to differ among individuals.

In my case, instead of trying to figure out whether I should aim for an annual income of US$50,000 or US$500,000, I can consider what sort of lifestyle I want to provide for myself and my family. While this ultimately requires a certain sum of money to support it, that amount will vary depending on where and when I live, how big my family is, and so on. Not only that, but also, as Warren Buffett demonstrates, the amount we earn does not have to directly inflate our lifestyle choices.

Since it helps to have a simple lifestyle measurement to apply, I've drawn inspiration from restaurant guides—you know, the kind that describe cuisine types, opening hours, contact details, and so on, followed by dollar signs symbolizing the price point of each establishment. Typically they range from one dollar sign ($) to four dollar signs ($$$$), but for our purposes, let's add a fifth ($$$$$) to represent a broader range of lifestyle choices.

Most people I know have a pretty clear idea where they fall when regularly eating out (by choice and not necessity). Maybe you'd rather grab a quick, simple meal at McDonald's, in which case, you may be satisfied with a $ lifestyle. On the other hand, you may prefer a three-star Michelin restaurant offering the finest wine selections from around the world—in other words, a $$$$$ lifestyle situation.

Say your family consists of a spouse and a ten-year-old son who really loves baseball. A $ lifestyle parent who wants to contribute to his fledgling baseball career might just play catch in the yard, or, at most, sign him up for a youth league at the neighborhood YMCA. The $ lifestyle provides the basics: love and support in a safe environment with enough to eat—and, for the most part, the rest is up to him.

Let's now consider the whole spectrum. If you're a $$ lifestyle parent, you might send him to a summer day camp. The $$$ lifestyle parent might hire a one-on-one coach from a nearby university, while the son of a $$$$ lifestyle parent attends a Major League Baseball (MLB) fantasy camp during summer break. Finally, the $$$$$ lifestyle level would look more like hiring a former MLB player to personally train your son. We've now gone from the baseball equivalent of McDonald's all the way to Wolfgang Puck.

This dollar-sign lifestyle system helps us to more easily peg our lifestyle preferences, including our Financial Baseline, typically established (or at least heavily influenced) by our early upbringing. For example, for the early part of my childhood in the US, our family depended on government aid. As such, my Financial Baseline sits at a modest $ lifestyle level.

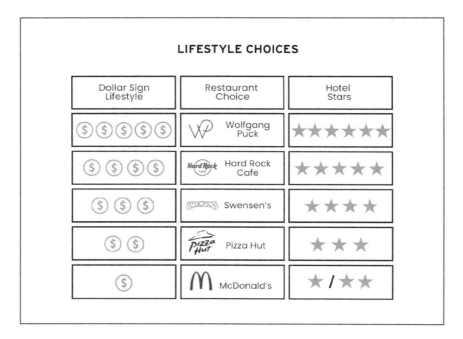

Financial Aspirations

So what shapes the Financial Aspirations that help determine how our lifestyles change over the course of our lives? Looking at my own lived experiences, as well as my basic understanding of human personality, I suspect two broad factors, including your North Star priorities and your personal financial drive in life.

Again, the North Star priorities represent the sources of long-term happiness typically rooted in one or two of the following: Serving Family, Serving Society, and/or Serving God. The specific constellation of your North Stars can help predict how you go about earning your living. For example, I may share the same primary North Star of Serving Family as my friend SY; however, our Financial Aspirations are different. That's because he has a stronger need to Serve Society (our common Polaris Ab) as compared to me. Although both SY and I forged careers in the financial services industry, he decided to take a huge income reduction and retire early—still in his early fifties—to teach part time and establish a photography nonprofit that donates money earned from his artistic passion to those in need.

Now, let's compare my insurance agent friend, Eleanor, with someone like Dietrich Bonhoeffer, a German Lutheran minister, theologian, and anti-Nazi dissident executed by Hitler's regime in 1945. Both share the same primary North Star of Serving God. However, while Eleanor's willing to make significant personal and financial sacrifices in service to God, she's less likely to risk violent death for her faith. We might further expect Eleanor to maintain somewhat higher Financial Aspirations than Bonhoeffer. While our admiration for Bonhoeffer rises into the stratosphere (deservedly so), that doesn't detract from Eleanor's sacrifices, nor does it say anything about Bonhoeffer's earning potential. Finally, we can also conclude that Eleanor's prioritized North Star of Serving God would result in a lower level of Financial Aspiration as compared to those of SY or mine (Serving Family).

The second factor I see influencing our Financial Aspirations is personal drive. Every individual seems to be wired differently when it comes to how much they're willing to work, and for how much pay. Even among myself and my three siblings—all raised in the same environment and sharing the same main North Star of Serving Family—you'll find different Financial Aspirations in terms of the lifestyle we aim to provide our respective family units.

So, what factors determine personal drive? While it's hard to pin down a conclusive answer, it's likely a combination of both nature and nurture. Research has shown that two nonidentical siblings only share about 50 percent of genes, all sequenced a bit differently and resulting in all sorts of varying physical and personality traits. That said, environment still plays a role. Even siblings growing up in the same home face vastly different life experiences, based on birth order, relative ages during major life events, peer groups they associate with, and so much more. For example, unlike my older brother, who hung out with his overachieving engineering cohorts in high school, a number of my high school friends didn't pursue a university degree. What's more, our three-year age difference meant that my brother and I experienced the trauma of war and relocation as refugees differently.

I'm no geneticist or sociologist, so I can't say more about *how* these dual forces of nature and nurture interact to form our different personality traits. However, it's clear that we're each motivated in different ways by different things, including when it comes to achieving professional or financial success—and that's okay.

There are no right or wrong levels of Financial Aspirations. We are who we are: a somewhat fluctuating combination of inheritance and experience. While we can get away from unhelpful influences, shift our thinking, and thereby increase our levels of drive (as I managed to do in early adulthood), there may be a limit to how much we can completely overhaul such traits. That's why we should honestly self-reflect and align our actions with our personal drive, as well as our respective North Stars.

Financial Values

I define Financial Values as the lifestyle trade-offs we're willing to make—directly or indirectly—when it comes to money matters. For example, I deeply value providing for my family (my primary North Star), and I managed to develop a strong professional drive. But that doesn't mean I'm willing to move away from or relocate my two young children in order to earn more money.

I've taken the previous example from real life, specifically the time prior to joining my most recent employer, when I was offered a lucrative opportunity to work in Hong Kong. The pay certainly appealed to me, and the company promised to take care of our home in Singapore—including maintenance costs—should I decide to relocate my family to Hong Kong for a period no longer than two years. This highly attractive compensation package, combined with the opportunity for rapid career growth, was quite tempting. Still, given my values around family, I couldn't justify the necessary sacrifices. The position's travel demands would cause me to miss out on even more time with my then-newborn son. Although I didn't fully realize it at the time, this decision to remain in Singapore would bring me closer to my chosen path.

As much as my Financial Aspirations would have appreciated the extra income, what was best for my family was for all of us to stay in

Singapore. While this may have meant sacrificing a dollar sign or more in my lifestyle rating, my Financial Values kept me in check—on the path toward my true North Star.

Financial Values also inform how we choose to carry out work duties. I've been fortunate in that, for most of my 30-year career in financial services sales—an industry and function often driven by commissions and bonuses linked to product sales—I've mostly worked for firms that prioritize their clients' interests. An exception to this became an issue with one of my previous employers when, after a senior management shake-up, I was directed to sell a financial product I felt was not appropriate. Forced to take a stand, I opted to present the product only to prospects and clients who were savvy enough to understand not just the potential for higher returns but also the high associated risks, which I clearly defined for them. This approach negatively impacted my bonus that year, as well as my career advancement within the firm under my then-manager. However, I needed to be able to face my clients, many of whom had become friends over the decades I'd spent in the industry. Needless to say, I resigned from that firm not long after the change in management and associated values.

Given that Financial Values and Aspirations are largely informed by personal experiences and external influences, we must recognize the impact of our digital world. Just as social media compounds "keeping up with the Joneses" related to Financial Aspirations, it can also distort our Financial Values. As parents, we need to make additional effort to spend quality time with our kids and ensure we pass on our values. After all, if we don't, someone else will.

As noted before, Financial Values should firmly align with our North Star priorities. This ensures we achieve the right balance between earning enough and protecting those values most conducive to long-term happiness. What's more, by modeling healthy financial habits for our families, we can better pass down our values to subsequent generations.

I'm aware that my bruised ego from the shame of childhood poverty and ridicule could tempt me toward a higher Financial Aspiration level, leading me to stray from both my North Stars and Financial Values. Avoiding these traps comes down to managing our egos and helping to promote proper lifestyle management—one that aligns Financial Aspirations and Values with our unique North Stars in a way that safely lifts our hot-air balloon into the skies and sustains its flight path.

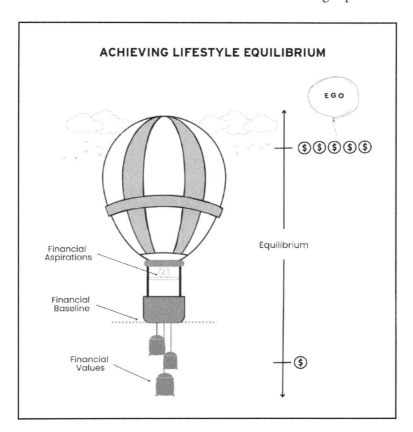

Next, let's examine how to do that.

IDENTIFYING LIFESTYLE AND INCOME LEVELS

Considering my family's refugee status and our related financial burdens growing up, I realize my Financial Baseline rests at the humble $ lifestyle level. My (perhaps overcompensating) personal Financial Aspirations alone—without any moderation—would probably bring me to at least the $$$$ level. If I'd stopped there, I may now be driving the BMW convertible my son saw at the mall. Perhaps I'd also work much farther away from my kids' extended family—and/or for a less client-centered firm—to earn more money. However, my focus on serving both family and society tempers my lifestyle needs. This combination of factors settles the score at around the $$$ lifestyle level.

It's my opinion that, once we're clear on our comfortable lifestyle level, greater income does not need to dramatically change how we live or spend. In fact, as Warren Buffett demonstrates, we shouldn't overextend our resources into extravagance just because we're earning more. Buffett's grounded philosophy and strong family ties impress me far more than any display of luxury or decadence (including fancy high-end BMWs).

Most of the time, when Financial Aspirations burn too hot, overinflate our metaphoric hot-air balloon, and send us flying unsustainably high, it's a clear result of a runaway ego intent on Serving Self.

It took me many years and a lot of growing up to realize that my urge to collect and display luxury items was rooted in the shame of growing up poor. In an effort to prove my worth, I poured my drive into earning, building first a financial safety net and then an armor of wealth around my bruised ego. I admittedly also developed a bit of a superiority complex around how much I worked, earned, and owned—that is, until I experienced the existential crisis that prompted my email to that vaguely paternal family doctor I hardly knew.

If you're struggling to come up with your dollar-sign number, I suggest a shortcut. If you were to travel with loved ones (and pay yourself) for a special vacation (not work trip) to a city with a cost of living comparable to where you live, where would you stay—a three-star hotel? Four stars? Once you have your answer, subtract one star, since we tend to spend above our lifestyle level when vacationing. The number you're left with most likely describes the specific lifestyle level aligned to your long-term happiness.

In my instance, my preferred hotel stay is normally a four-star hotel. Subtracting one from the four hotel stars would reduce it to a three, equating to my having a $$$ lifestyle.

With our lifestyle dollar-sign number in hand, we can easily convert this into a dollar amount that we need to sustain it. For example, if you have a $$ lifestyle, you would likely choose to own or rent a home in a nice working-class neighborhood. One dollar sign above that, you would choose to own a home in a middle-class neighborhood. At a $$$$ lifestyle, you'll likely purchase a home in an upper middle-class neighborhood that comes with a highly rated school district. You may also decide to send your children to private schools.

I chose housing expenses for this exercise because it represents the highest household cost item for most of us. With each respective lifestyle choice, you can add in other expense items such as cars, vacations, dining, and so on. Totaling these up and adjusting for your taxes and pension contributions will get you to your estimated income dollar amount required to cover your lifestyle expenses.

Whether you end up with three dollar signs or three and a half, it really doesn't matter—and there's no need to split hairs. What matters is that you understand why you chose your number and how to arrange your lifestyle accordingly to optimize long-term happiness. For me, that number led me to forgo the convertible BMW 6 Series for a modest lower-end European sedan (a considerable step up from the bicycle and bus commutes of my childhood).

It is my hope that both of my children will grow up to find their respective dollar-sign numbers—ones that reconcile their Financial Aspirations and Financial Values centered around their respective North Star priorities. As Warren Buffett has demonstrated, happiness depends far more on our North Star values than on fancy dinners, cars, or houses.

I trust that by not trying to compete with the "Joneses" of the world, E and S will learn that earning money is not about displaying the fanciest objects, but about nurturing what matters most to each of them individually.

TAKEAWAYS

Finding the amount of money that brings personal contentment isn't about striving to outearn your neighbors or proving your self-worth through conspicuous consumption. It's also not about reaching some annual income figure universally associated with optimal happiness. Ultimately, it comes down to finding the lifestyle level that aligns with your own Financial Aspirations, Values, and, most importantly, your own personal North Star priorities. Understanding these aspects of yourself can help you make financial and professional choices so you feel both satisfied and secure—minus the insatiable ego hunger or regret.

At the end of the day, we must be willing to give, as well as take. Meanwhile, like Warren Buffett, we must learn to appreciate what we have and enjoy—whether reliable cars or McDonald's lunches—without worrying so much about outearning or posturing for others. Above all, we need to recognize our true sources of long-term happiness, our North Star priorities, then align our Financial Aspirations and Values—and our lifestyle choices—accordingly.

As a parent, I realize how our values and belief systems—as well as our unhealed insecurities—can get passed down, not just to our children but also to all the generations that follow. Therefore, it's our responsibility as parents to honestly reflect on our own relationships with money. This provides us the Financial Values needed to temper the flames of our Financial Aspirations so we can safely lift ourselves and our families up—without the whole balloon crashing down. In this way, we can adjust to new realities while always supporting those core values that bring happiness to ourselves and others.

LEARNING POINTS

- "Keeping up with the Joneses" will keep you forever trapped on the hedonic treadmill.

- Your preferred *lifestyle level* is determined by your Financial Baseline, Aspirations, and Values.

- To maintain perspective and balance—and achieve lasting happiness—align your Financial Aspirations and Financial Values to your North Star priorities.

- Beware being led adrift by your ego and giving into lifestyle creep.

SELF-REFLECTION

- When traveling with loved ones for pleasure, do you stay at a five-star hotel, a two-star hotel, or somewhere in between? This helps determine your preferred lifestyle level ($–$$$$$).

- Can you recall moments when ego led you to spend beyond your means? If yes, what do you believe fed your ego?

PART 2
INCOME

4

WHAT IS A JOB?

You should not confuse your career with your life.

—Dave Barry

The first and last time I aimed an F-bomb at a direct supervisor was in the earlier part of my career in Asia. My then-manager, Dave, and I were circling the final phase of a protracted negotiation with a South Korean financial institution. I was 34, brash, and arrogant. After I landed in Hong Kong six years earlier, my career had taken a steep upward trajectory. With no stable relationship or family of my own, work consumed my life.

Dave, meanwhile, was by far the most family-oriented senior professional I'd encountered, before or since—a rarity in the financial services industry.

I'd been thrust into a complex transaction almost immediately after starting at the firm. It began in Hong Kong, where I'd wake before dawn to brief Dave, who was based in Australia, on the previous day's discussions and determine next steps. Then came an all-day session, from breakfast until well after dinner, with only a short break for lunch. This exhausting routine repeated every day for about a week before I traveled to the South Korean capital of Seoul. There, Dave met me in person for a final week of negotiations. By that point, I was fully wired on caffeine and nicotine.

As we moved toward our deadline, I learned that Dave planned to return home *before* the scheduled date of the document signing. His son had just graduated from high school and would soon leave for his postgraduation trip overseas, so Dave wanted to be there to send him off.

Fair enough, I thought—until I learned that his son's flight wouldn't depart until the Sunday after our transaction closing date. When he clarified that he wanted to attend a going-away party scheduled several days before his son's flight, I lost my patience—and, I now realize, all perspective. I'd spent close to two weeks living and breathing this deal, and here was Dave, ready to bail before the ink even hit the dotted line. For his kid's *party*.

This led to my telling Dave—using certain choice words I have never since repeated to a manager—just what I had thought of his decision to prioritize his homelife.

Just one year after that heated exchange, I found myself disillusioned and disoriented, considering a career change to pursue my passion or join another firm that would sacrifice pay for greater perceived "purpose and meaning." So, I asked for advice from that good doctor I'd recently met—who insisted I had it all wrong.

Your job, he advised, is nothing more than a means to that end.

"That end," of course, was my source of long-term happiness— whatever that meant to me at the time. I would never have guessed back then that Dave and I shared the same primary North Star. While he'd figured it out, I was still trying to equate happiness with climbing the corporate ladder.

With this backdrop, let's take a hard look at jobs: what they are, where they came from, and where they're going. What key developments in our rapidly changing global marketplace shape how we perceive and approach jobs today—and how does that good doctor's advice fit in?

A BRIEF HISTORY OF JOBS

According to Dictionary.com, a job is "a piece of work, especially a specific task, done as part of the routine of one's occupation for an agreed upon price." *Merriam-Webster* defines it as "a regular remunerative position."

There's something elegantly straightforward about these definitions. They don't claim a job should deliver happiness, realize life's purpose, or fulfill one's passion. Jobs simply require us to trade time and effort for money. We hint at this definition when asking what someone does for a *living*. In short, we work to live—not the other way around.

However, these definitions differ from (or even outright contradict) how many seem to view jobs today—namely, as some default centerpiece of life that somehow trumps other aspects.

To understand how we got here, let's review a brief history of jobs in the United States. Again, why focus on the US? I've found that most research and public debate about work seems to start there, before spreading to other parts of the world.

America's first colonies largely adhered to so-called Protestant ethics of hard work, frugality, and contributing to society. However, when compared to other historically Protestant European countries, such as Germany, the Netherlands, and those forming Scandinavia, we see stark differences in how a number of those values have been applied (or not) over time. These European nations had invested in generous social benefits like universal healthcare and had successfully shifted toward greater work-life balance. America, meanwhile, has doubled down on *hard work* even as runaway consumer spending and relatively weak social safety nets suggest that *frugality* and *contributing to society* have declined.

As I write this, the US remains the world's only advanced economy where workers are not legally guaranteed even a single day of paid time off (PTO). *Forbes* reported in 2023 that almost one-third of American workers lack access to PTO, and more than half with PTO end up working during their "time off" anyway.[1]

This is hardly news. In 1992, Juliet Schor, an American economist and sociology professor at Boston College, wrote *The Overworked American*. This book reports that Americans have outworked other industrialized Western nations since at least the early 1970s.

There seems to be a disconnect in America when it comes to the *living* part of "making a living." The 2023 *Forbes* article previously noted opens with an explanation of why American small business owners with no legal obligation to offer PTO might do so anyway: PTO can "raise [workers'] morale and improve their productivity." In short, PTO may help employees *work* better. Not a word about improving workers' lives outside of avoiding burnout from work.

IT'S ALL ABOUT THE BOTTOM LINE, RIGHT?

Do longer working hours result in more money in the pockets of American workers? Not so much. As Americans blur the line between their work and personal lives, philosophical concepts like *purpose*, *meaning*, and *passion* increasingly saturate US job postings, mission statements, and other recruitment and HR trends. At the same time, average take-home pay for American workers has remained fairly stagnant after adjusting for inflation.

How do we reconcile this apparent trend toward mission-driven work—even as we observe more and more employers prioritizing profit over workers? What, if any, are the risks of viewing work this way? Once again, it helps to zoom out and examine how jobs have evolved over time.

Industrialization

Before the Industrial Revolution, most workers in Europe, the United Kingdom, and Westernized colonies and former colonies—including in America—worked as either farmers or artisans. This means they enjoyed direct contact with tangible results of their work. As a carpenter, you might spend all day in your workshop, but at the end, you'll have a new chair built with your own two hands. This direct connection to the fruits of one's labor meant that some sense of meaning and pride (not to mention, dopamine-boosting gratification) was naturally built into the work itself. Let's call this direct connection *meaningful work*.

This direct link could (and still can) be found for some professionals, such as physicians and nurses, some engineers and skilled trade workers, and the like. For many, though, industrialization severed the direct connection between what workers did and what they produced. Instead of spending all day building a chair, they worked on an assembly line, building just one small part. As the world embraced machines, people themselves became cogs in a wheel, working long hours—usually amid unsafe conditions—well into the 20th century.

It wasn't until the 1930s that the Fair Labor Standards Act in America improved working environments and banned practices like child labor. Most workers subsequently gained evenings, weekends, and holidays off—along with pension plans to support themselves and their dependents after retirement. Meanwhile, industrialization brought about more affordable goods and services to the average worker.

By the end of the 20th century, employers were adding suggestion boxes and implemented employee recognition programs to boost engagement. Many remained disconnected from the tangible fruits of their labor, spending days working, not just on assembly lines, but also now in retail, customer service, or in abstract corporate support functions like finance or human resources (HR). But at least they could enjoy time off and feel basically safe (maybe even appreciated!) at work. Plus, they could look after their families (what I see as the true centerpiece of life for most of us) and plan their retirements. These changes forged a mutually beneficial pact between employers and employees.

That is, until "the perfect storm" came.

The Perfect Storm: 1980s

In 1980s America, a few factors aligned. First, we started seeing the effects of the 1974 pension reforms. Originally meant to protect employee pension funds, these reforms started a trend away from corporate-defined *benefit* pension plans, which required companies to pay their employees' retirement benefits until their death, in addition to supporting their dependents.

Defined benefit pension plans soon gave way to defined *contribution* plans, such as 401(k)s and IRAs, where employers and employees could both pitch in contributions (although employer contributions, including matched rates, are not mandatory). Compared to defined benefit (DB) plans, employers offering defined contribution (DC) plans no longer have to pay lifelong benefits to their retired workers. This shift reduces potential company liabilities that can distort their financial results. However, as we'll see, DC plans come with serious side effects for a majority of employees who lack the knowledge, interest, or time when dealing with investment-related activities (see Chapter 7).

Then came policies used to stimulate business growth, and thus job creation and entrepreneurship, by lowering taxes for high earners. During President Ronald Reagan's eight years in office, the federal personal income tax rate dropped from 70 percent to 28 percent for those in the top marginal income bracket.[2]

Dubbed Reaganomics, these economic policies went further by reducing federal regulations on businesses. The idea was that the government should get out of the way, since company leaders and shareholders could be trusted to do the "right" things—while maximizing profits. Then, more profitable companies would invest their additional gains and hire more workers—so everyone wins! Besides, lower taxes would mean more wealth in the hands of people able to spend it, spurring further economic growth through what was termed "trickle-down economics."

Those of us who lived through the 1980s in America may recall that it was often referred to as "the decade of decadence." This was the heyday of Wall Street, as shareholder values surged and the term "private equity" began to appear in the lexicon of mainstream media—including the 1987 hit film *Wall Street*, starring Michael Douglas as corporate raider Gordon Gekko.

Who could forget Gekko's signature line, "Greed, for lack of a better word, is good"? This seemed to have been the era's unofficial mantra, as taking over companies and laying off workers, and/or selling off parts of businesses to maximize shareholder value became acceptable—even applauded.

The old employment model, that of loyally working for one company and then collecting a pension, was over.

The focus on maximizing shareholder value also encouraged the outsourcing of jobs to cheaper locations overseas. "Corporate rightsizing" to reduce costs became, and still remains, the norm for a large number of American companies. These practices succeeded in growing company profits and shareholder value. While they can create jobs, it's less certain that this still-growing concentration of wealth has spurred a significant trickle-down effect—especially among working Americans who have seen both job and retirement security diminish. In fact, it's caused what I'd like to refer to as a "trickle-out" effect as companies outsource manufacturing and other supply chain labor to lower-cost developing countries, putting even more money into the pockets of shareholders and executives.

These developments place a lot of pressure on Americans to set up their own financial security, which I believe helps fuel the country's workaholism and its ideal of rugged individualism over collective values.

There's cause to wonder whether this obsession with self-reliance, plus increasing financial insecurity, has contributed to worse mental health outcomes in the US. According to a 2002 study led by Mark Olfson of the New York State Psychiatric Institute within the College of Physicians and Surgeons at Columbia University, the rate of outpatient treatment for depression in America skyrocketed starting from the latter part of the 1980s. The study found that between 1987 and 1997, the number of outpatient treatments for depression increased by over 300 percent.[3]

To understand whether this trend continued beyond the period between 1987 and 1997, Olfson and Steven C. Marcus of the Philadelphia Veterans Affairs Medical Center conducted a follow-up study for the ten years immediately following (between 1998 to 2007). The follow-up study found that the rate of outpatient treatment for depression saw a modest level of increase, but not as significant as that found in the earlier decade.

Would it then be surprising to learn that unemployment leads to depression? According to a 2009 article published by the Institute for Work & Health, "There is clear evidence that becoming unemployed has a negative impact on mental health."[4]

While correlation does not always mean causation, it's been my experience that people are more susceptible to depression when they begin losing hope for the future—and when this happens, short-term sources of hedonistic happiness more easily draw them in, especially in the consumer-driven American marketplace.

This phenomenon led Schor (author of *The Overworked American*) to publish a 1999 follow-up: *The Overspent American*. In this second book,

Schor explores (surprise!) the "keeping up with the Joneses" effect. This book examines the socioeconomic causes and impacts of two diverging trends in the late twentieth century: "upscaling" (the dominant trend of Americans spending above their means) and "downshifting" (the relative minority shirking this trend by spending less). Based on her research, Schor claimed that, compared to upscalers, downshifters tended to choose "more meaningful work" and live "much happier" lives—namely, ones "that line up squarely with their deepest values."[5]

Job-Related Traps

Through this perfect economic storm of the 1980s, we saw the rise of corporate policies that eroded employee job and income security—despite the fact that Americans work longer hours than employees in most other developed nations. As I researched these issues, I noticed a connection between these trends and two major job-related traps in the US and, increasingly, elsewhere.

The first has to do with something called "enmeshment," which occurs when personal boundaries between people or groups dissolve. The term was first used by family therapist Salvador Minuchin to describe relationships in which personal boundaries have become unclear, leading one or both individuals to lose their sense of self. This happens when one begins taking on the emotions, views, or goals of the other person. As we'll see, people can become enmeshed at work either by tying their identity to their job status, or role.

This leads us to the second job-related trap, that of looking for life purpose and meaning directly through work. As my doctor acquaintance sees it, the healthiest way to view a job is as a means to an end.

He argues that jobs only indirectly support happiness by helping us serve our core values and afford our lifestyles. They're not meant to completely define our identities or provide our lives with some ultimate deeper purpose.

ENMESHMENT AT WORK

The phenomenon of professional enmeshment, found often among senior executives, is rooted in tying one's identity and self-worth to work. Even when the initial reason for adopting this mindset emanates from the need to provide for family, this singular focus on one's job can have unexpected and dire consequences both to one's family and to other aspects of a person's life.

Although I later tried to root my career into my newfound provider role as a father, to my younger mind, work remained my primary gauge of personal "success," which I measured by titles, pay grades, and promotions. I went on to become the workaholic father who told himself he strove to support his family while, in reality, getting distracted by the false North Star of Serving Self. It took the COVID-19 pandemic and subsequent lockdown for me to realize just how much precious time I'd missed at home.

According to Janna Koretz, a psychologist who works with high-pressure professionals, the combination of high achievement, intense competitiveness, and a culture of overwork can lead to enmeshment at work.

In 2019, Koretz observed in the *Harvard Business Review* that "the work culture in many high-pressure fields often rewards working long hours with raises, prestige, and promotions."[6] When employees spend most of their time involved in an intense activity, that activity begins to influence or even define how they see themselves. This makes them more likely to work harder, sacrificing even more time with family or other personal pursuits. Indeed, some companies seem to implicitly encourage employees to postpone family life altogether by offering fertility benefits like egg and sperm freezing programs and in vitro fertilization.

Even if you never marry or have children, what happens if you tie your identity too closely with your work? Marc Schulz, co-author of *The Good Life*, points out that people who too closely identify with their careers and job titles are more likely to suffer a crisis of identity or self-worth in retirement.

It makes a lot of sense to me: One day, you're a well-respected senior executive, and the next day you're left struggling to figure out who you are. Especially for those who have either neglected or failed to build meaningful relationships outside of work.

Traditionally observed among senior executives, enmeshment has become more widespread across various ranks of an organization.

SEEKING PURPOSE AND MEANING THROUGH WORK

The second common trap seems to be growing more prevalent, especially among younger generations: pursuing life's meaning and purpose directly, sometimes primarily, through work itself. For me, this meant basing my career choices on how closely my personal values matched the perceived or alleged values of the hiring companies. I've since learned (the hard way) that corporate mission statements don't always align with reality. Especially when management changes.

Still, workers increasingly look for purpose and meaning through work. In 2023, Sander van 't Noordende, CEO of the global staffing and HR services organization Randstad, reported on this through his "Workmonitor" study of more than 30,000 employees spanning Europe, Asia Pacific, and the Americas. He found that not only do "workers today want the whole package from their employers: secure, flexible, inclusive, and financially stable employment," but also, "over half of the people in our study would resign if they felt like they didn't belong or have a sense of purpose."[7]

Furthering this point, a study led by Shawn Achor (the author and happiness researcher referenced in Chapter 1) and published in 2018 found that a shocking majority—nine out of ten people—reported a willingness to take a *23 percent reduction* in their future lifetime earnings in exchange for "a job that was always meaningful."[8] While these results held true among different age and salary groups, the trend seems to be growing among the younger cohorts.

Is it then surprising to learn that researchers, HR professionals, and consultancy firms increasingly emphasize the importance of corporate "purpose" to attract and retain workers? This conversation has been going on for decades. Back in 1989, authors Perry Pascarella and Mark Frohman published *The Purpose-Driven Organization*. The book makes the case for corporate "purpose" as a key driver of creativity, innovation, and employee commitment/engagement.

More recently, in 2014, John Mackey, co-CEO of Whole Foods Market, and Raj Sisodia, a former professor at Bentley University in Massachusetts, published a book called *Conscious Capitalism*. They argue that capitalism can and should serve a higher good—not just for the benefit of shareholders who invest in company stocks, but also for everyone: customers, employees, suppliers, and the environment.

This idea seems to also be catching on among corporate leaders. At a Business Roundtable in 2019, 181 CEOs of leading American companies signed a statement that proclaimed "While each of our individual companies serves its own corporate purpose, we share a fundamental commitment to all of our stakeholders." One such commitment cited was "investing in our employees."[9] To me, the true test is whether these CEOs are willing to take actions to benefit the purpose(s) they espouse even when those actions detract from shareholders and their own financial interests. This includes how willing they are to lay off employees to boost or maintain stock values in instances where profitability remains unchanged or even increasing.

Both of these job-related traps make employees more vulnerable to exploitation at work. It's not hard to see how professional enmeshment and the pursuit of meaning and purpose through work are interrelated—and how both can benefit employers at the expense of employees. When workers dedicate their whole attention to work, this can drive productivity and, therefore, higher profitability for the company. It can also make employees easier to manipulate into overextending themselves, even as worker income security plummets.

Finally, when workers devote too much time and energy to their work, it often comes at great cost to their personal lives. A *Journal of Management Studies* paper co-authored by Anna Jasinenko and Josephina Steuber published in 2023 drew some interesting conclusions.

The co-authors referenced existing studies that found "employees who perceive too much meaning and purpose in their work face the risk of neglecting private and family responsibilities (Bailey et al., 2019; Dempsey and Sanders, 2010, Oelberger, 2019). In turn, this neglect bears the risk of negatively affecting their well-being at work and in general (Haar et al., 2014; Lantau et al., 2014)."[10]

MAINTAINING PERSPECTIVE

If, according to *Merriam-Webster*, a job is a simple "remunerative position"—just *the means to an end*—why then has the subject become so complex and all-consuming? Why do so many companies tout some (often disingenuous) "higher purpose" in their corporate mission statements? Finally, why do so many younger professionals demand these elements from their careers and employers?

To me, it has to do with either failing to recognize or losing sight of our North Star values. While I believe most people find lasting happiness through Serving Family, it's easy to misinterpret what that means. For example, we can get overly fixated on becoming a financial provider. This can cause us to spend too much time away from home or become exhausted and emotionally unavailable to those we're meant to serve.

True Meaning and Purpose

Too many workers, in the US and around the world, have come to conflate "meaningful work" with "finding meaning or purpose through their work." Earlier in this chapter, I defined "meaningful work" in terms of the relationship between what we do in our jobs and what we produce. The artisan furniture maker and spinal surgeon both experience a direct link between their labor and its tangible results, which instills greater inherent meaning to their efforts, compared to an assembly line worker, retail worker, or customer service agent.

Am I arguing that there is no greater meaning or purpose to be found at work? Certainly not. Like most things in life, finding healthy fulfillment at work is a nuanced matter not easily summed up in absolutes (see Chapters 7 and 8 on the role of passion in our work).

However, when it comes to discerning the difference between seeking meaningful work and seeking meaning *through* work, it helps to know your true North.

For example, a physician who sees her profession primarily as a calling to heal has found work that's personally meaningful to her. She may even feel inclined to occasionally sacrifice family time or take a reduced income in order to provide care to underserved populations. However, there may come a point where the sacrifices are too frequent and she begins neglecting essential family responsibilities. Crossing that line means that she's shifted from meaningful work to living her meaning through her work. She needs to get clear about her true North: whether it is Serving Family or Serving Society/God.

Even when she is clearly serving her true North, the physician may find that she's not doing meaningful work. Imagine a scenario where that same physician gets placed in an administrative role at a large medical services company. Even with a pay raise, she suddenly finds herself less fulfilled as the gap widens between her labor and its direct impact on patients. The greater the distance between these two points, the less meaningful the work.

Finding meaningful work is important. In the case of the hypothetical physician, clinical service will bring her far more professional satisfaction than an administrative role. The trick is maintaining perspective and balance so she doesn't try to seek life's meaning and purpose solely, or even primarily, through work itself. This easily leads to enmeshment or exploitation. Even the most charitable and devoted physician can still maintain professional boundaries so that her work does not detract from her primary North Star. Unless, unlike the majority of us, her true Polaris A is either Serving Society or Serving God.

Purposeful Firms

Recruiting corporations who push "company purpose" and lofty mission statements might be sincere—or maybe they're marketing themselves to appeal to the growing wave of employees looking for greater meaning through work. I would personally lean toward the latter. In particular, be wary of any company that leverages employee commitment to company purpose to encourage longer working hours or excessive travel that further disconnects workers from their families and home lives.

"Company purpose" as I define it is the *primary* reason for an organization's existence, beyond and separate from shareholder profits. For example, a social enterprise may set up a chain of cafés that provides jobs for those with disabilities, or a firm could offer business loans to impoverished communities. However, these organizations' primary reason for existing is not profit.

I believe that socially and environmentally conscious for-profit firms do exist—just not at the level one might expect, given all the mission statements, "core values," and "company purpose" buzz out there. Meanwhile, true social enterprises and nonprofit options often don't pay enough to comfortably care for a family, especially at higher lifestyle levels.

Further, Jasinenko and Steuber found in their study that company purpose (beyond profits), as a concept, faced several key issues. These include "the lack of a clear construct definition, measurement tools, and empirical testing of optimistic prospects in prior research on organizational purpose."[11]

Even among nonprofits and social enterprises, mismanagement and fraud is always a risk. While I suspect most of these entities truly aim to benefit society, many professionals I know in the nonprofit world admit they find their work less meaningful than expected, especially when poor management or workplace bureaucracy comes into play.

Avoiding the trap of Serving Self through chasing status can protect us from becoming enmeshed at work. I know from personal experience how easy it can be to focus on career growth to the expense of family. After all, developing and sustaining personal relationships can get messy. Work, on the other hand, can offer comparatively clear expectations and a greater perceived sense of control. Meanwhile, devoting oneself to the provider role can feel productive even when it's become a distraction from what truly matters. Choosing a company for its reported values can lead to major disappointment, especially given that values shift each time management changes hands.

I count myself lucky in terms of the impact of the COVID-19 lockdowns. Being forced to stay home provided the opportunity to reevaluate the value (or the lack thereof) that I placed on time spent with my two children. I'm particularly grateful that, unlike O'Kelly and others, I was able to see and correct this mistake before it was too late.

After realizing I was miserable within that Hong Kong–based job—the one that started with me cussing out my supervisor—my next career move was indeed aimed at increasing my sense of purpose through work. When the opportunity came to work for a company that felt more aligned with my values, I jumped, despite a large cut in both pay and status. It seemed that no one in my life at the time understood why I would do such a thing. That would have included the old doctor who explicitly warned me against "looking for happiness" directly through work.

Now, years later, I realize he was right. I'd wanted an escape from my unfulfilling life, and I thought I might find purpose in working for a company that shared my values. If I could find that, I thought, I'd wake up each morning excited to go to work. My life would be complete.

Unfortunately, that was not the case. I truly was, in the good doctor's sentiment, looking for happiness in all the wrong places.

TAKEAWAYS

It shouldn't surprise anyone that in *Chasing Daylight*, Eugene O'Kelly's position as CEO and chair of one of the world's leading professional services firms didn't factor much into his final days. Like most people who know they're dying, O'Kelly had more important things on his mind—namely, his family and loved ones.

The irony is that we know this. We all do. Yet so many of us still choose to focus on climbing the corporate ladder or killing ourselves to chase some start-up success. After all, we have deliverables—not to mention bills—and (as far as we know) most of us are not currently moving through our final days.

The point is that we have to maintain perspective when it comes to seeking purpose and meaning through work to avoid becoming enmeshed in our jobs. Yes, some companies do pursue purpose beyond profits. And yes, some jobs are more inherently meaningful than others, depending on how you define that for yourself. However, not everyone will easily find a company or job that provides both. Even less likely—at the income level required to comfortably sustain themselves, their families, and their desired lifestyle level.

It could be that you come from a family with intergenerational wealth. Or your primary North Star happens to truly be Serving God or Serving Society, and your work aligns with those core values.

For most of us, though, maybe a job is just that—a job. A means to provide us income to support what truly does provide purpose and meaning: building stronger families and societies. If you ask me, that's a much safer bet for sustaining long-term happiness.

All of that said, it remains vitally important to earn enough—and, as this chapter points out, corporate trends have reduced both job and income security for many people in the US and around the world. Unless we find a sustainable way to take care of ourselves and our families financially, all of my philosophizing will ring hollow and this book won't amount to much more than a paperweight. I can already see how quickly the job market has changed since I was a young professional, and that change seems to be accelerating.

LEARNING POINTS

- Unless your primary North Star is Serving God or Serving Society—and your professional role aligns with that guiding core value—work represents a means to an end and not the end in itself.

- Late 20th-century American economic reforms, which influenced trends around the world, have reduced job and retirement security for most workers.

- *Overidentifying* with or defining your worth through your professional role/status can lead to unhealthy *enmeshment* at work.

- For most, trying to find your life's meaning and purpose through your work can distract you from your true North Star path of Serving Family and negatively impact your well-being.

SELF-REFLECTION

- Would you feel like you lost your identity if you lost your job or retired?

- How can you find work that's personally meaningful, without letting it define your life's overall meaning and purpose?

5

INCOME SUSTAINABILITY IN THE NEW ECONOMY

In today's uncertain economy, the safest solution to be wealthy, be in total control and enjoy freedom for you and your family, is to have multiple streams of income.

—**Robert G. Allen**

In 1930, John Maynard Keynes, known as the founder of modern macroeconomics, claimed that by 2030, most people would only need to work 15 hours a week, thanks to technology, machines, and new ideas.

This prediction has not aged well (to say the least). Rather than enjoying increased leisure time, most American employees remained tied to a 40-plus-hour workweek throughout the 20th century—and to this day. Our recent increased digital connectivity means that, for many employees in the US, work now bleeds into evenings, weekends, and even vacation time.

Keynes's optimism made him an outlier among his contemporaries and those prior. Since the dawn of the Industrial Revolution, new technologies have sparked anxiety about machines displacing workers. In the early 19th century, some workers sabotaged machines to defend against job losses in England. In China during the late 1880s, the Qing dynasty opposed the construction of railroads, fearing the decline of luggage-carrying jobs.

Now, almost a century after Keynes's failed prediction, we're seeing another surge in tech advancements—dubbed the Fourth Industrial Revolution (4th-IR)—poised to disrupt the marketplace. In particular, white-collar workers worry that rapidly developing artificial intelligence technologies could make their skills obsolete, impacting everything from content creation to data analysis.

I recently brought this up over lunch with a friend, the CEO of a global financial services company in Singapore. His eyes lit up as he whipped out his phone to show me how he's begun automating his personal content marketing. As an active LinkedIn user, he previously sent drafts of his posts to his marketing department for review. Now, he uses LinkedIn's AI-powered writing tools to help him both generate and edit posts instead.

We next discussed how lower-cost countries can leverage AI and other tech tools to provide even cheaper and more efficient support to companies in higher-cost countries. Over this past year alone, I've spoken to a number of professional services companies in Singapore that are looking or continue to outsource a number of white-collar middle-income roles to lower-cost Southeast Asian countries.

While the World Economic Forum expects a significant change

in the types of jobs resulting from technological advancements, analysis by the worldwide management consulting firm McKinsey and Company ("McKinsey") suggests that the number of middle-income jobs are expected to see the greatest decline. As new technologies shift how the world works, how can we prepare ourselves and our children to earn sustainably?

In trying to understand the nature of income sustainability in a rapidly shifting global workplace, I find it helpful to differentiate among three different ways of earning income and the mentality that accompanies each one, including Employee Mindset, Entrepreneur Mindset, and Investor Mindset.

Let's dive into the implications of the 4th-IR, as well as strategies for income sustainability moving forward including each of the earning mindsets I just introduced, what we can learn from each, and even how to begin preparing ourselves and our children to think more like entrepreneurs and investors.

But first, let's take a quick look at some predictions about the future and lessons from the past.

THE FUTURE AND HISTORY OF EMPLOYMENT

As I investigated what future job markets might look like, I found that, in four key ways, forecasts from differing sources more or less align.

The first point is that **technology's rate of change will continue to accelerate** as new breakthroughs create an exponential growth in both new developments and their speed to market. In a 2021 report, McKinsey forecasted that "in the next decade, we will experience more progress than in the past 100 years, as technology reshapes health and material sciences, energy, transportation, and a wide range of other industries and domains."[1]

Secondly, **the number of net new jobs resulting from technological advancement will be positive**, despite a large number of expected job losses. According to the World Economic Forum's *Future of Jobs Report 2023*, "the impact of most technologies on jobs is expected to be a net positive over the next five years."[2]

The third point is that **the income gap could continue to widen** between high-earning and low-earning workers. In its *Jobs Lost, Jobs Gained* report published in 2017, McKinsey wrote, "Our analysis shows that most job growth in the United States and other advanced economies will be in occupations currently in the high end of wage distribution. Some occupations that are currently low wage, such as nursing assistants and teaching assistants, will also increase, while a wide range of middle-income occupations will have the largest employment declines."[3] The report predicted that income polarization could continue, barring policy choices such as increasing investments in certain sectors.

Finally, **displaced workers will need help**—likely from governments working together with corporations—to recover income losses and reskill displaced workers for new roles. In the same 2017 report, McKinsey claimed that "income support and other forms of transition assistance to help displaced workers find gainful employment will be essential."

There's little reason to doubt that technology's rate of change will continue to accelerate. From artificial intelligence (AI) to e-commerce to gene sequencing, we've already seen an exponential rate of new developments from one generation to the next.

Looking back, we can also see that, as workers and companies adapt, rapid technological advancements tend to eventually yield increased prosperity, including a net increase in new jobs as the marketplace evolves. For example, sharp declines among agricultural and manufacturing jobs in the 20th century coincided with an overall growth in employment afforded by new technologies—including, in recent decades, computers and other digital advancements.

However, even as the volume and variety of new jobs both increase, the income gap may still grow, likely to have a disproportionate impact on middle-income workers. Over the past 100-plus years, labor unions and other formalized workers' rights movements have emerged in developed markets like the US and other western nations as they industrialized. Unfortunately, we've seen a reversal in the level of worker protection over the last four-plus decades in America.

Even as they went through their own industrialization journeys, most emerging markets offered a fraction of the worker protections found in the US (what is left) and other developed nations. Could it be that these developing countries are drawing from the American playbook? As a result, we now see vast inequalities when it comes to wages and workers' rights around the globe, despite a more industrialized and connected world. The countries hit hardest tend to rely more heavily on the informal sector—loosely defined as those workers without formal contracts or protective benefits like social security or paid time off for sickness (or any other reason).

Aside from the impact of technology directly on jobs, I bring all of this up, first, because I expect to see more employers in developed markets like the US and some European and Asian markets, replace full-time hires with contractors. Secondly, since the 1980s, we know that the US has trended away from worker protections and promoted policies that privilege company leaders and shareholders. Both of these factors can lead to the outsourcing of jobs from higher-cost to lower-cost countries. Since so much of both the developed and developing world takes cues from American market patterns, there are likely serious implications for the future of jobs anywhere.

So why would the world's most powerful economy still actively promote Reagan-era policies that reduce income and job security, and increase an already dire wealth gap that's depleting the middle class? I point to two broad reasons: 1) an emphasis on maximizing shareholder value and 2) a general lack of empathy among policy makers and those who have amassed exceptional wealth from recent technological developments.

I'm not arguing that capitalism is bad. Nor am I supporting any form of socialism or communism. I'm simply observing that, from the perspective of a finance professional intimately acquainted with both Western and emerging economies, I know what happens when contract work and offshore outsourcing increase as both market regulations and worker protections erode. Unless something changes, I suspect that in developed countries such as the US and the UK (and others that follow their policies, including a number of developed countries in Asia), wealth gaps can and will increasingly resemble those seen across the developing world.

In fact, I expect to see a repeat of the mass layoffs experienced by middle-class, blue-collar manufacturing workers in the US and the UK that began in the 1980s. The only difference this time around is that it will be the middle-class, white-collar workers—in developed countries that do not prioritize employee interests—who will feel the brunt of the layoffs.

When it comes to how or even whether governments and corporations can work together to better support and reskill displaced workers in these shareholder-focused economies, I'm not overly optimistic. It's simply that I don't believe such efforts will do much to reverse the growing income and wealth gaps in the US unless different policies are adopted—ones that better balance the interests of shareholders with those of workers, among other stakeholders. However, I do see some cause for optimism when looking at how more socially conscious nations have developed successful alternative models of capitalism.

Even if one can't escape needed worker redundancies, appropriate policies can still help to cushion the blow to affected employees. Sweden, for example, maintains a capitalistic, free-market economy. Albeit slightly outdated, a BBC article published in late 2019 reported that as a result of the large number of organizations established to get retrenched workers back to work, about 90 percent of laid-off workers in Sweden (based on OECD data) were back to work within one year.[4] In exchange for charging its citizens higher income tax rates, Sweden offers other generous social benefits related to healthcare, higher education, child day care, ample pension support, and more.

Meanwhile, Switzerland—a nation that consistently ranks among the top ten happiest countries globally, along with its Nordic and other historically Protestant European neighbors—provides healthcare subsidies for those who can't afford the premiums for mandatory basic insurance. Insurers are not allowed to make a profit from their basic insurance offerings, although they can earn profits from supplemental insurance plans. They're also barred by law from refusing coverage based on age or medical condition.

In short, whether world leaders choose it or not, it seems at least possible to preserve a free-market society without adopting the extreme "greed is good" capitalism of the US and UK during the early 1980s that continues today.

Frankly, I don't expect this more balanced, sustainable approach to capitalism to catch on in the US, UK, or here in Asia anytime soon. As such, it's up to us as workers and parents to adapt our mindsets accordingly and find our own paths to income sustainability in the new economy.

Now, let's dive into those three mindsets, beginning with the most common and familiar: the Employee Mindset.

THE EMPLOYEE MINDSET

Most early impressions about work and unofficial job training for kids take place in K–12 school. After that, students may go on to select a major and study four years (or more) at a university.

What do most people do after that? They go look for a job, hoping all that schooling has adequately prepared them for the marketplace. But what kind of training do we actually get at school?

Traditional schools have long been institutionalized. We divide students into strict age-based groups, impose mandatory schedules and rules, and measure each student's performance according to standardized rubrics. There are some good reasons for this, including socialization and measuring learning outcomes in a scientific way. However, I believe this highly rigid structure also serves to ingrain the externally imposed, rule-following employee—without sufficiently exposing students to either invest or launch/manage their own business.

For our purposes, I define this as "Employee Mindset."

None of this is bad, per se. We all benefit from having a society with rules, feedback, and logical outcomes. However, I believe that ongoing technological and policy trends will make it financially necessary for most people to also engage in investment and/or entrepreneurial activities. I also see that even those individuals who still choose to work for someone else should develop a mindset of lifelong learning and adaptability—just to keep their salaried jobs. In short, innovation and adaptability are necessary ingredients of success going forward.

In the past, employers likely benefited more from a deferential, loyal, and complacent Employee Mindset. Factories, for example, needed workers to stay in their lanes, follow directions, and mainly perform repetitive, predictable tasks. For centuries, most workers specialized in specific, narrow skill sets—whether as a farm laborer, typist, or clerk—and dutifully executed those roles throughout their careers.

These days, employers want more versatility and adaptability from workers. They may still value compliance and loyalty to some extent, but they also increasingly need employees who can perform a wide range of tasks, help them strategize, and pivot on a dime—especially as technological change continues to accelerate, constantly transforming how we approach and execute business. Otherwise, these employers will themselves fail.

Meanwhile, a lot of jobs that seemed stable may soon become obsolete. Professional drivers, for example, may be replaced by self-driving vehicles. A lot of content creation can be outsourced to (or at least assisted by) AI software. Even medical and financial professions see unprecedented change. Decades from now, will people still see their general practitioner for medical problems, or will most doctor visits get replaced through telemedicine and either diagnostic or treatment technologies we can't currently anticipate? How do we help ensure income sustainability as these trends accelerate?

The Role of Education

Educators know the workplace is changing. They understand their students may end up in careers that haven't yet been dreamed up yet. So, how has the field of education shifted in response?

According to what I've gathered from my educator friends, as well as from some basic research and observations, I'm noticing a few trends:

Increased emphasis on STEM (science, technology, engineering, and mathematics) subjects.

Focus on training a "growth mindset" that emphasizes lifelong learning, rather than a more static approach to developing and executing a narrow skill set.

Enhancing "soft skills" that encourage continuous learning to complement STEM skills, especially the so-called four C's of *collaboration*, *critical thinking*, *creativity*, and *communication*.

Prioritizing resilience and adaptability, to prepare students for an increasingly changing marketplace.

STEM EDUCATION

Today, the basic coding knowledge of many middle and high (secondary) school children far exceeds what I was taught in college. Even beyond specific tech skills, like coding, a solid STEM education trains critical thinking and logic that can be applied to everything from CGI animation to developing clean energy technologies. The financial world, for example, now shows a significant preference for new hires with a firm understanding of the scientific method and process-based learning, which helps them analyze investment opportunities and markets.

GROWTH MINDSET

The concept of the "growth mindset" emerged in the first decade of the 21st century, popularized by Carol Dweck, a Stanford psychology professor, whose research focused on motivation, personality, and social development. In her 2006 book, *Mindset: The New Psychology of Success*, Dweck argued that most successful people believe that their success comes not from some innate ability (fixed mindset), but rather from hard work and continuous learning (growth mindset). According to Dweck, this helps explain why successful people are less likely to fear failure and more likely to view setbacks as opportunities to learn and adjust course.

THE FOUR C'S

The "four C's" mentioned previously—collaboration, critical thinking, creativity, and communication—were first introduced by Israeli author and history professor Yuval Noah Harari, in his book *21 Lessons for the 21st Century*. Harari contends that students are best prepared to deal with a constantly changing and technology driven world by teaching them to work together (collaboration), negotiate different perspectives (critical thinking), innovate new solutions (creativity), and clearly express and advocate for themselves (communication).

RESILIENCY AND ADAPTABILITY

According to the United States Bureau of Labor Statistics, the average American worker in 2022 stays on a job for only 4.1 years.[5] In the same year, Zippia (an online recruitment service) found that millennials stay in a job for less than three years (2.8 years).[6] While it's hard to give a definitive reason for this trend toward shorter tenures, whether job changes result from terminations, layoffs, or employee choice, the implications remain the same: Workers should expect to adjust to multiple job changes throughout their lives.

For decades, psychologists and public health experts have ranked job loss among the most stressful life events, along with death of a loved one, divorce or separation, moving, and long-term illness. Even voluntary job changes are often accompanied by relocation stress, not to mention the necessary onboarding and retraining process.

Limitations of Pedagogy

As a parent of young children, I appreciate educational trends that help young people gain important STEM-related and "soft" skills, in addition to qualities like resilience, adaptability, and a pattern of lifelong learning.

However, this instruction takes place within a system that, by default, largely trains the Employee Mindset.

What happens when students make the leap from this familiar classroom environment to a marketplace increasingly driven by contract work and constantly transformed by accelerating technological change that challenges income sustainability?

Will they know how to pivot after a layoff or contract termination?

Can they retrain themselves to shift from one mode of business to another to keep pace with technology?

More to the point, can workers shift from simply relying on earning all their income from traditional jobs to building sustainable and diversified income streams from investing or operating a business?

THE ENTREPRENEUR MINDSET

According to a poll conducted by National Public Radio and the Marist Institute for Public Opinion, about 20 percent of US workers worked as independent contractors in 2018.[7] In a similar report from McKinsey in 2022, that number appears to have grown, with 36 percent of American civilian workers representing independent workers (although this later study included temporary employees, freelance workers, and gig workers).[8]

If history has taught us anything about how companies prioritize shareholder interests in the US and elsewhere, we can safely expect the number of contract workers to continue to increase, as well as more jobs to get outsourced to cheaper labor in foreign markets. Indeed, a 2020 study by Intuit, a business software company specializing in finance, found that more than 80 percent of large US corporations plan to substantially increase their use of a flexible workforce, providing management of these companies higher levels of efficiency, agility, and flexibility.[9] While, in the past, the outsourcing of jobs in the US mostly affected blue-collar workers in the manufacturing sector, current trends seem on track to impact large numbers of white-collar jobs.

Just-in-time Labor (Contractors)

This brings to mind the concept of a "just-in-time" (JIT) system borrowed from Japanese auto manufacturers decades ago. Basically, this term describes the practice whereby companies receive inventory as close as possible to when they're needed. This differs from the traditional model of stocking up on-site inventory, which proves inefficient and wasteful due to the high cost of storage and ongoing shifts in product demand.

Now, as we move from an economy rooted in manufacturing to one more driven by people, the JIT approach can be similarly applied to human capital. Rather than paying for expensive benefits and retraining employees to keep up with changing marketplace trends, companies can instead rely on a combination of automated technology solutions and a revolving door of independent contractors from all over the world.

I can easily envision a world where a number of companies will use this model. Perhaps by the time E and S are ready to launch their careers, employers will maintain only C-suite roles, along with select senior level and highly specialized staff—otherwise relying on JIT labor solutions for most of their remaining employment needs. Under this model, a university graduate skilled in computer programming will likely enter the workforce not as an entry-level employee, but as an independent contractor navigating a very different world: one in which she must provide her own insurance and other benefits, while constantly hustling for her next client or contract.

In addition to instability of income and lack of benefits, contract workers, especially those who find work through intermediaries, lack insight into their client company's strategic plans. Contract workers also lack access to employee training provided by human resources departments to protect against skill obsolescence. These risks will become more apparent as the rate of corporate outsourcing continues to rise, hopefully prompting contract workers to get resourceful when educating and training themselves to protect against skill set obsolescence.

"True" Entrepreneurs

What I'm describing is really nothing more than a more formalized gig economy. While this form of independent contracting offers more flexibility in terms of setting hours and managing workload, it comes with major drawbacks in terms of benefits, income security, and skill set obsolescence—especially in a 4th-IR setting.

I recently spoke to an Australian friend, also named Philip, who founded a Tokyo-based executive search firm. He made an interesting observation about the distinction between many people who work for themselves and what he defines as "true entrepreneurs." Gig workers, independent contractors, solopreneurs, and even business owners, he says, simply apply their existing skill sets.

Those who continue to rely on their existing skill sets will remain largely vulnerable to sudden market shifts. For example, what would happen to Uber, Lyft, or long-haul drivers when self-driving cars and trucks took over? Just like salaried bus drivers, these workers will be out of work and forced to learn new skills.

Philip argues that the difference between those who continue to rely on existing skill sets on one hand, and those with a true Entrepreneur Mindset on the other has to do with the ability to identify unmet or underserved market needs and innovate new ways to meet those needs. According to him, it isn't enough to simply become a business owner, contractor, or gig worker to survive in the emerging new economy. You have to be able to not just react to market changes, but also become an *active driver* of such change. To do this, you need to be able to experiment, innovate, and—above all—have enough faith in your ability to take on trying a completely new approach. As such, the true Entrepreneur Mindset requires not only risk tolerance, but also the ability to anticipate and strategize new business models and adjust skill sets accordingly.

Meanwhile, until a few years ago, I had never been anything other than an employee and investor. Then, in 2021, I began developing an app to help English-speaking children in Singapore to more efficiently retain and recall Chinese vocabulary. This required me to incorporate a small business.

Imagine my surprise when Philip observed that he sees me as more of a true entrepreneur than someone like himself. As he explained, "All *I* did, mate, was take the current skill set I developed by working at a headhunting firm, hang up my own shingle, and hire people to do the same. What *you* did, on the other hand, was to identify a problem—English-speaking Singaporean students having trouble remembering Chinese vocabulary—and create a totally new resource utilizing psychology tools to help solve that problem."

It occurred to me then that much of my success as an employee also came down to this habit of identifying complex problems and experimenting with novel solutions, albeit within the context of my job. In other words, the true Entrepreneurial Mindset not only leads to greater success both within and outside of traditional employment, but also will become increasingly necessary to sustain income, whether you're an employee, a contractor/gig economy worker, or company owner. In short, we need to redefine the Entrepreneur Mindset beyond the traditional conception of owning and running a business—especially when we consider the risk of changing client needs and skill set obsolescence.

THE INVESTOR MINDSET

When you ask most people about how they earn money, they'll talk about what they do for a living, whether that's working a job for someone else, self-employment as an independent contractor, or running a company. Few respondents bring up being an investor. However, having worked in the financial industry my entire career, I've noticed that a far greater proportion of the wealth generated by companies gets funneled to reward shareholders versus compensating company workers. That trend has only continued its rapid growth since the 1980s, contributing to increasing income and wealth inequalities that continue unabated in the US and globally.

This made me curious. Does the data support this assertion? I started to dig into the research.

Rewards to Shareholders (Asset Owners) vs. Employees

In 2019, the Roosevelt Institute (an economic think tank) published a working paper authored by Lenore Palladino looking to explain the correlation between stagnant middle-class wages and the focus on maximizing shareholder value observed in the US that began in the 1970s.

Palladino's paper referenced a 2015 study by Mishel and others, which found that for about three decades after World War II, the real hourly compensation of most workers in the US grew in line with productivity growth. Thereafter, however, real wages have not grown in proportion to productivity. Instead, wages have fallen as a share of national income.

Palladino also referenced the works of free-market supporting economist Milton Friedman, who penned a 1970 essay published in the *New York Times*. Friedman argued that a company's greatest responsibility lies in satisfying its shareholders. He reasoned that corporate spending on socially responsible activities (including those that favor the position of workers) amounts to a tax on shareholders.

Friedman characterized corporate executives as mere shareholder agents, insisting that all decisions about spending on socially responsible activities should rest solely with shareholders. As such, a corporate executive's sole objective is to return as much money to shareholders as possible, the latter of whom can then vote with their conscience as to the social cause(s) they choose to support. This view, termed "shareholder primacy," maintains that the purpose of any corporate action should primarily, if not solely, support maximizing wealth for shareholders.

According to studies by Greenfield in 2018 and Lazonick in 2014, this philosophy of maximizing shareholder wealth began to influence actions of executives and board of directors of companies. After all, shareholders can replace both executives and directors if these "agents" don't act in shareholders' perceived best interests.

Moreover, shareholders can apply incentives to reward executives and directors for acting in their interests. Unsurprisingly, we saw a subsequent increase in the percentage of CEO compensation come through direct stocks and stock-related awards in the US. In 2023, a paper by Josh Bivens and Jori Kandra of the Economic Policy Institute found that by 2022, stock-related pay accounted for slightly more than 81 percent of top CEO realized compensation.[10]

As a result, shareholding awards to top CEOs saw their compensation increase disproportionate to that of workers between 1978 to 2022, according to the same Bivens and Kandra paper. Studying total pay data of the US's largest listed firms, the co-authors found that compensation of top CEOs increased by 1,209 percent compared to 15 percent for the typical employee (adjusting for inflation) over this period. Their research also showed that in 2022, top CEOs were paid 344 times (realized compensation) as much as a typical worker, compared to 21 times in 1965.

Lastly, I found a 2022 working paper from the National Bureau of Economic Research titled "Shareholder Power and the Decline of Labor," which further supports Palladino's assertion. Its co-authors, Falato, Kim, and von Wachter, found data pointing to the increase in a company's percentage of institutional ownership (a steady and rising trend since 1980) with its simultaneous reduction of employment and payroll expenses. A possible explanation for this phenomenon is that the higher the concentration of power of shareholders, the more they can directly influence the actions of CEOs and board of directors. Such actions, meant to maximize shareholder value, can end up hurting the position of workers.

We can all imagine scenarios where company management and board of directors opt to cut employee expenses to benefit shareholders by laying off workers and/or outsourcing to cheaper workforce in or outside of the US. Of course, other reasons, such as decreased antitrust enforcement and the reduction in the number of unionized workers, are also possible contributors to worker interests taking a back seat.

Fighting for Scraps

Whether or not there's conclusive evidence supporting a direct *causal* relationship between rising rewards to shareholders and a relative stagnancy in worker pay, the trends for both are clear. I simply argue that we should not just be preparing ourselves (and our children) to fight for financial leftovers as employees.

So many parents spend inordinate time, effort, and money on their children's formal education designed to train them for employment with companies. This fails to position children for a marketplace that privileges shareholders over employees' basic job security, let alone financial reward.

While I'm a proponent for formal education, I believe it's also imperative to teach ourselves and our children to adopt an Investor Mindset—not just in our retirement accounts, but also as part of an income diversification strategy. In recognition of this need, I'm teaching my children at an early age to invest with the help of a financial advisor.

THRIVING AMID INCOME UNCERTAINTY

I recently heard the phrase "raise the child in front of you" from a former colleague describing her own parenting approach. This resonated with me, given my desire to customize my advice to honor both of my children's unique aptitudes, areas of interest, and personalities when guiding them toward becoming happy, thriving adults.

While this applies to all aspects of parenting, the question of how to guide children toward professional success, including sustaining income, particularly stands out to me. Even if I could accurately predict what skills will be in demand when my children reach working age (which I certainly cannot), what happens if their aptitudes and interests don't align with these marketable skills of the future? As a parent, I don't want to push my children into an area of study or work that they won't enjoy or feel ill-equipped to compete within.

On top of that, much of my early professional drive felt rooted in a hunger that grew out of the survival mindset of my childhood. On observing my children's relative lack of drive to survive (and hearing the same concern among other parents living in Singapore), I worry that their cushy upbringing will fail to instill that hunger, resulting in lower professional drive. I understand that early struggle is not a prerequisite for career success. Also, as the family therapist reminded me, I know that I can't get my kids to see the world through my eyes. My point is simply that it's not always easy to look past your own assumptions to provide the right support, especially across generations. So, how can we advise and support our children and others who lack interest or aptitude for 4th-IR-driven fields so they don't get left behind in the new economy?

Although a practical approach is to teach our kids to adopt both an Entrepreneur and/or Investor Mindset, many parents I've spoken to fret over how to help their children adopt either one, especially while they themselves still rely on traditional jobs as their main source of income. I get it. In the past, I've questioned how much such skills can even be taught.

However, the way my friend Philip defines the true Entrepreneur Mindset—as one focused on curiosity and strategic problem-solving, which can be applied across all forms of work—gives me hope. It's also promising that schools and workplaces increasingly focus on training the growth mindset introduced by Carol Dweck. In my opinion, when you combine the practice of constantly asking questions with Dweck's focus on hard work and continuous learning, you'll naturally hone the ability to identify needs/problems and then how to meet/solve them.

Meanwhile, it's becoming increasingly necessary to supplement earned income with market assets. Unfortunately, the Investor Mindset is not something most teachers or parents tend to prioritize when preparing children for the future, even though many parents I speak to agree that it's important.

While we need to prepare our children with all three mindsets (Employee, Entrepreneur, and Investor), we shouldn't assume that it'll be an *easy* journey, especially if we've not embarked on similar ones ourselves. I hold the view that we need to "walk the walk" if we want our children to embrace such lessons. This was one of the reasons I took time away from writing this book to start my first business venture. I made the same conscious decision to start a joint investment account for my two children. I further try to actively involve them with both, from having them select a few of the stocks in their joint portfolio to asking for their feedback on my business venture. While they're hardly experts in either matter, I want them to get exposure to both.

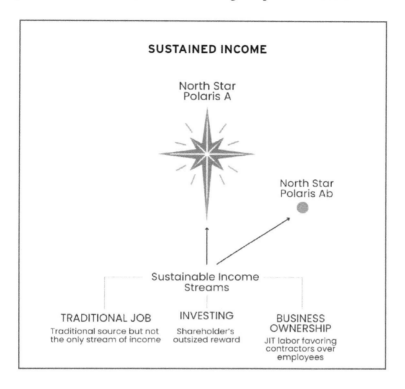

Finally, I believe we should be cautious of binary advice often dished out by financial gurus and influencers without taking into account the inclinations and circumstances of the individual receiving the advice. Many of these experts advise against traditional employment altogether, arguing that you'll never get rich working for someone else. Instead, I suggest taking a more nuanced approach that considers the appropriate ratio of income sources for each individual.

For example, one of my children may end up working full time as an employee or contractor, while doubling this earned income through investments. The other may develop an entrepreneurial zest, earning 70 percent of their income as a business owner and the remaining 30 percent from investments.

I don't know what John Maynard Keynes would have to say about how things turned out or where we're heading next, but I don't believe that the 4th-IR will have us working a few hours a day while otherwise enjoying abundant leisure time.

If history is any indication, middle-class white-collar workers in developed countries that do not prioritize workers will likely suffer considerable income disruptions, requiring them to incorporate some degree of investing and/or entrepreneurialism to sustain their livelihoods. The competition will come not only from emerging technology but also from those from lower-cost countries.

To increase our chances of sustaining our income and thriving in the 4th-IR, we must adopt some elements from the Employee, Investor, and "true" Entrepreneur Mindsets to create our own, personalized strategies for financial independence. And in the unlikely event that something like Keynes's prediction comes true, adopting a more adaptive, problem-solving mentality and a diversified portfolio of income streams can still benefit us.

TAKEAWAYS

We now understand that the old model—going to school, earning a higher degree that specializes us to perform a specific job until retirement—is no longer enough to get us where we want to go. We talked about how to earn enough money to support our preferred lifestyle for ourselves and our families, while staying true to our North Star values. If that's the "end" we're pursuing, we're going to need a more dynamic, diversified "means" to that end—more than just a traditional job, that is.

To achieve this, we should think more in terms of a portfolio of income sources, including investments and opportunities for business ventures. Those who keep pace with and benefit from market changes will likely be more tech savvy, lifelong learners with the ability to identify and solve problems, regardless of how they earn.

Of course, every single individual is different. Just as we all have different constellations of North Star values and lifestyle levels, we also have different aptitudes and interests that help determine which financial mindsets come more naturally to us. Though I believe we need to adopt all three mindsets, it's unrealistic for someone with a low innate drive or level of interest in running a company to become even a moderately successful business operator.

The key, as I explain to my own kids, is to move away from the core assumption of "I need a job" as the only or primary means of generating income. The new economy looks different. It's determined by rapidly changing technology, HR trends like just-in-time (JIT) labor, and an increasing global income gap largely benefiting asset owners and senior executives. To move beyond a survivor mindset to one of thriving, we all need to develop and optimize some unique proportion of all three mindsets, according to our own set of inclinations and circumstances. While the first mindset is taught in school, the other two are not.

So how do we help our children go beyond simply adopting the Entrepreneurial and Investment Mindsets to taking action? That question will be addressed shortly, based on my three-decade-plus experience of working in the investment industry and my shorter, more recent time as a small-scale entrepreneur.

Rather than assuming we need to first cultivate certain traits in order to branch out as an investor or entrepreneur, it's more important to take that first step toward building a more integrated mindset of financial independence—irrespective of our innate traits or inclinations.

LEARNING POINTS

- In today's uncertain and rapidly changing work environment, adopting the traditional *Employee Mindset* is no longer enough to thrive.

- Since the 1980s, US companies increasingly funnel the greater share of profits to shareholders, while employee wages have largely stagnated—and these trends will most likely continue or even accelerate.

- Even for traditional employees, succeeding in the new economy requires developing a "true" *Entrepreneur Mindset*—one that adapts to change, identifies market needs, and innovates solutions.

- A portfolio of income-generating investments and business ventures can contribute to sustainable income going into the 4th-IR, especially in countries that prioritize shareholder gains at the expense of other stakeholders.

SELF-REFLECTION

- How is your area of work likely to be affected by the 4th-IR?

- Do you already possess a "true" Entrepreneur Mindset—and if not, how can you develop a more adaptive, innovative approach to identifying and solving for needs in the market moving forward?

6

THE FINANCIAL INDEPENDENCE MINDSET

If money is your hope for independence you will never have it. The only real security that a man will have in this world is a reserve of knowledge, experience, and ability.

—Henry Ford

In the mid-2000s, I accompanied my friend Mike on a business trip to Shanghai, a gorgeous metropolitan city bisected by the Huangpu River. On one side, skyscrapers and neon lights dominated a dramatic, contemporary skyline. The other side featured the more traditional style of the Bund, marked by colonial European architecture preserved from the former Shanghai International Settlement. The purpose of Mike's return to this bustling financial capital of China? To expand his property portfolio and for me to get started on mine.

I had doubts, however. First, I told Mike I'd run my analysis of the units we viewed to estimate the rate of return. While the results presented an attractive return, I decided against investing anyway, explaining that I didn't know enough about the country's tax policies, or whether foreign currency control limits might complicate my ability to get money out of China.

The look on Mike's face made it clear he didn't buy my arguments. He countered every concern I raised and corrected some false assumptions. More to the point, all indications suggested that the section of Shanghai in question was poised to experience a real estate boom second to none.

In short, Mike moved ahead, and I chose to walk away. More than 15 years later, Mike's Shanghai investments have made him a small fortune—while I continued working my nine-to-five job and depositing my comfortable salary and bonuses at the bank.

With the clarity of hindsight, it's easy to regret missed opportunities like this. It's much harder to figure out why we hesitate. Looking back, I had all the right information, plus a credible and trusted advisor. Mike's analysis of the opportunity was right on most, if not all, counts. Just a couple of years prior to this Shanghai trip, I'd taken the plunge as a first-time home buyer, driven by a growing desire for roots—for a place to truly call home. Unfortunately, having taken that step in buying a first home in Singapore did not help spur me to action when it came to an investment property. My interest in the first property was deeply personal, while the other involved the risks and uncertainties that come along with business ventures and investing.

Given the feedback I've received, it seems I'm not alone. I've spoken to many people who experience similar reluctance when it comes to building a comprehensive investment portfolio or starting a business. So how do we overcome the initial hurdle of getting started?

This question led me to examine factors related to both Entrepreneur and Investor Mindsets, and, more importantly, what makes us hesitate to take that elusive first step. Thus, I began the journey to explore whether such hesitancy exists, and if so, what can be done to overcome it.

BEYOND ENTREPRENEUR AND INVESTOR MINDSETS

Revisiting that missed opportunity on the Huangpu River prompted me to recall some advice I heard during a business trip to New York City about 20 years ago (around the same time I declined to invest in Shanghai). Jet-lagged and unable to sleep, I'd been watching a CNBC segment featuring the popular financial planner Suze Orman.

If my memory serves me, a call came in from a young woman who had just received a relatively modest inheritance. This caller wanted to know how to manage her windfall so that, when she became a mother, she could choose to stay at home with her children instead of working.

The straight-talking advisor replied that the caller simply hadn't inherited enough, nor did she have sufficient time for her money to grow.

How I interpreted what Orman said next left a lasting impression on me.

She urged the caller to stop thinking about "financial independence" as some targeted sum of money that, once achieved, allowed you to sustainably pay for lifestyle expenses without having to work.

This got my attention because that was exactly how I defined the term at the time. I had even created a spreadsheet to track the amount I thought I needed to accumulate before I could safely quit my Hong Kong job and do something I enjoyed.

It made a lot of sense to me. Any amount of money can be lost through poor investment outcomes, inflation, fraud, or even major, uninsured medical procedures. Instead, one should view financial independence as a mindset. Paraphrasing her description from memory—*the belief that no matter what happens to you or your surrounding circumstances, you'll always be able to provide financially for yourself and your family*. This to me also meant losing a job—the major, if not sole, source of income for a large number of people.

If anyone embodies that "Financial Independence Mindset" I took away from that CNBC segment, it's Mike. Specifically, Mike always had a mindset focused on generating income outside of traditional work, either through investing or starting a business, or both.

It helps that Mike came from a family of entrepreneurs. Most parents I talk to agree that background plays a part, including the fact that most of us are institutionalized by school to pursue traditional jobs as our sole or primary source of income. While our different upbringings likely contributed to the mindset difference between Mike and me, I suspect there was more at play. After all, as I mentioned in Chapter 5, I managed to develop what my friend Philip described as a true Entrepreneur Mindset when it came to identifying problems and innovating solutions (albeit applied through most of my working life as an employee).

In terms of the Investor Mindset, it's clear that Mike has always understood the outsized benefits of owning stocks and properties. Throughout my career in finance, I've helped many individuals and organizations grow their wealth through such asset ownership. I, therefore, also share Mike's Investor Mindset.

What puzzled me was this: If I already possessed both the "true" Entrepreneur and Investor Mindsets, what then explains our different choices on the shores of the Bund those years ago?

My conclusion? There must be factors beyond these two mindsets that prevented me from taking that first step toward investing, let alone starting a business venture. In short, there's a big difference between understanding (and even beginning to adopt) the right mindset—and actually turning that mindset into reality.

Could it be that our individual circumstances act as obstacles preventing us from stepping out of our comfort zones and taking action? Let's explore this question.

OVERCOMING OBSTACLES

In the earlier chapter, we looked at how developing Entrepreneur and/or Investor Mindsets can help us avoid ending up on the wrong side of a growing wealth gap. In short, thinking beyond the Employee Mindset will be critical for ensuring income sustainability moving forward.

From my three decades working in the investment management industry, I know how often people talk themselves out of golden opportunities—like mine in Shanghai. Many similarly struggle to take the first step of starting an investment portfolio, much less regularly monitoring and actively managing their assets. Despite my decades of experience in the financial industry and awareness of the importance of the Investor Mindset, I shared some of that reluctance until more recently.

Think of it this way: If 100 people who now work as traditional employees picked up financial best sellers like *Rich Dad Poor Dad* by

Robert Kiyosaki or *90 Rules for Entrepreneurs* by Marnus Broodryk—and read them to the end—how many, who understood the advice imparted, would go on to actually apply what they learned? When I asked this question to my friends and colleagues, the most optimistic response I got—even from the successful entrepreneurs and investors I spoke to—was about 20 percent. The more pessimistic estimates range between 1 percent and 5 percent.

I came to realize that the inability to take that first step is extremely common among those of us who've been institutionalized into the Employee Mindset through a combination of education, modeling from parents with traditional jobs, and years of working for others (often while paying down debts and never putting our regular income at risk). This conditioning holds tremendous sway over us, even those of us who are able to simultaneously develop or already possess the Entrepreneur and/or Investor Mindsets (at least in terms of intellectual understanding).

Curious about why this is, I began meeting with financial planners, investors, entrepreneurs, and peers to gain insight into how they viewed or explained this phenomenon. All were happy to share their experiences of investing and/or starting a business venture, including what led to success or failure. However, no one could elaborate on the factors that could act as barriers to taking that first step, beyond reasons that are commonly cited.

I did, however, notice three main categories of responses cited among those I spoke with. Most of these individuals—especially those from families already operating a business or actively investing—never experienced that initial hesitation; they simply did it. A few started their business ventures out of necessity—they couldn't find employment at the time and needed to pay the bills. Some subsequently continued on with their businesses while others returned to the traditional workforce. The remainder joined their families' existing businesses.

Since these folks couldn't shed light on the "first step" problem, I began looking for books that targeted the apparent majority of people—those who felt unable to overcome their initial reticence—and was unsuccessful in finding any. Every year, you can find a number of newly released books on how to build wealth through investing in financial instruments and property, but those books seem to serve the narrow minority of people already comfortable doing such things.

Eventually, I found a study jointly published by the Behavioural Economics in Action at Rotman and the Behaviourally Informed Organizations examining two groups of people who failed to act on their financial plans.[1]

The first group represented those who would like to get plans but failed to do so. The second group, which the report primarily focused on, comprised those who received a financial plan but failed to follow through.

The study listed 11 reasons why these groups stalled out: procrastination, too many choices, conflicting goals, lack of salience in benefits, ambiguity, information complexity, unsure of procedure, problem is too distant, benefits are too vague, fear of unknown, and something called "licensing effect," roughly defined as the sense that people's past achievements, earnings, or good deeds somehow exempt them from making further efforts.

Next, I pored over material about what stops people from starting their own business. From blogs by entrepreneurial coaches to *Forbes* magazine, I noticed some main points, such as fear of failure and difficulty in getting funding or finding customers. Secondarily, people pointed to poor planning, aversion to hard work, and lack of stability.

However, I began to ponder whether the reasons cited for hesitating to either start an investment portfolio or a business venture were symptoms or causes.

For example, when someone procrastinates, I can come up with two potential explanations. The first is that the person lacks interest in the activity. How many of us have experienced firsthand the habit of repeatedly moving certain items on our to-do list to the bottom due to disinterest? The second could be that there is a lack of urgency due to not properly assessing the seriousness of a situation. Take, for example, someone who keeps putting off purchasing life insurance—until they learn of a relative's death, which spurs them to action. To me, this simply comes down to an issue of risk assessment.

Next, let's look at the fear of failure when starting a business. First, we need to separate out financial and nonfinancial fear of failure, the latter of which is outside the scope of this chapter. As for fearing financial failure, couldn't we attribute this ultimately to access to financial resources? If I fail in this business, will I have access to financial resources in order to pay my rent or feed my family?

I also frequently hear that this fear of financial failure is not something younger people should be concerned with since they're often advised to take risks while they are still in their early years. While there may be a few exceptions, this advice is only true if the young person can move back in with her parents or can couch surf with friends until she recovers financially. For someone who may not have support from family or friends, the same luxury of doing either is absent.

By focusing on causes (rather than symptoms), I began to notice three common themes that they fall into: lack of clarity about one's goals, risk assessment (and the role of optimism), and dealing with uncertainties.

Let's unpack those three points next.

Clarity of Goal

When it comes to true clarity of goal, it helps to revisit some essential personal questions: *why, who, what (+how much)*, and *when*. If we want to take action to apply our Financial Independence Mindset, we need to self-reflect in order to understand our individual motivations.

For me, the answer to *why* and *who* is the same—my primary North Star of Serving Family.

What has to do with generating sustainable income, which of course begs the follow-up question of *how much*. To answer that, I can cite the preferred $$$ lifestyle level I strive to provide for my family.

The final question of *when* will be addressed in the final part of this book, which explores the precise nature of the "Passion Gap" and how long it takes to close it. I define this gap as the amount of sustained income needed to satisfy our lifestyle choice while allowing us to pursue our passion (without necessarily needing to rely solely on a traditional job for income).

When we can answer these basic personal questions, we can better clarify our goals, plan strategies, and increase our chances of success.

Of course, there will always be people whose clear goal is simply to accumulate as much wealth as possible—sometimes even at great cost to themselves, their family, and society. This book, however, is not written for these individuals but instead for those seeking to align their earning efforts with service to their North Stars.

Keep in mind that you don't have to become a billionaire, or even a millionaire, to find "success." There are plenty of investors and business owners who have defined—and achieved—success in more modest terms. If we set more realistic goals, based on our personal lifestyle preference and grounded by our true North, we'll also face much higher chances of sticking to the plan and achieving our goals. Not all of us will (or should) adopt a "go-big-or-go-home" philosophy when setting our financial goals.

Risk Assessment (and the Role of Optimism)

When financial advisors determine the risk profile of an investor, they assume a long-term holding period of at least one full market cycle (generally five or more years). Although all advisors worth their salt also educate investors about the benefits of riding out at least one market cycle, far too many novice investors (or those lacking interest) nevertheless panic and exit their investments as soon as they see the markets experience a significant dip.

What's more, these investors most likely reached out to their advisors or invested in the first place when markets were strong, out of either excitement or fear of missing out.

Buying high and selling low is the exact opposite of what you're supposed to do. This disconnect between the recommended buy-low-sell-high model in *theory* and the tendency of inexperienced/uninterested investors to nevertheless reverse this model in *practice* leads to inaccurate risk assessments for them. But what contributes to this disconnect?

In the 30-plus years I've worked in the investment industry, I've yet to see a meaningful solution to this common issue. The trend persists in spite of attempts by advisors to educate investors about the benefits of playing the long game. Current approaches to assessing risk tolerance tend to instead blame this pattern on short-term reactions to fear or greed, especially among less savvy and uninterested investors. While I don't disagree, let's dig a layer deeper. Perhaps the better measure of risk tolerance comes down to that old question: *Is the cup half full or half empty?*

In other words, how naturally inclined are you toward optimism or pessimism, especially when things go wrong—like a significant dip in the stock market? This will largely determine how well you can handle risk, especially when those risk levels land on the higher end.

As we know, solid investments and business ventures should be viewed as long-term opportunities, despite shorter term variabilities. However, these short-term ups and downs can cause serious anxiety to the more pessimistic among us, prompting us to cut our losses at inopportune times. As such, it is my opinion that any good long-term measure of risk should prioritize, or at least consider, this personality trait.

There's no single right or wrong answer to the optimism-pessimism question, and every individual should make an honest self-assessment on this front. That said, it's best to temper both extreme optimism—that overconfidence that you will (or should) always get the outcome you want—and, on the other hand, a defeatist mindset that stops you before you can even start. Too much optimism can lead individuals to cavalier risk-taking (often very costly) and a lack of due diligence. But when pessimism leans defeatist, the result is nonaction. We've all heard the saying "if you don't play, you can't win," which certainly applies here.

If the optimism-pessimism spectrum does represent at least a *somewhat* fixed aspect of personality, it could serve as a helpful measure of an investor's risk tolerance when it comes to playing the long game.

Optimists are more likely to ride out market volatilities, keep their sights set on the longer term investment horizon, and therefore reap the benefits of the stock market. By their very nature, optimists are able to see beyond current circumstances to glimpse some light at the end of the tunnel.

Pessimists, meanwhile, tend to see every loss or obstacle as evidence of an increasingly negative slippery slope. Their minds envision worse-case scenarios: "The stock market has dropped a lot. This could lead to a recession, which could mean losing my job and not being able to pay my mortgage. I should just cut my losses, liquidate my investment portfolio, and save it for the rainy day that's sure to come."

When you're constructing a portfolio or starting a business venture, I suggest using your optimism-pessimism outlook profile to help assess your risk tolerance. If you're an optimist, you're much more able to ride out periods of high market volatility. If you lean toward pessimism, it's better to take a low-risk approach to building a portfolio or establishing a business venture.

Regardless of where you fall on the optimism-pessimism spectrum, I'd like to make one thing clear: You can construct an investment portfolio and/or start your own business. While some may claim that only optimists can get past that first step and find entrepreneurial or investing success, I maintain that both avenues are open to anyone—you just need self-awareness about your own risk tolerance, as well as clear answers to those basic questions (*why*, *who*, *what*, *how much*, and *when*) and, as importantly, the ability to deal with uncertainties.

Dealing with Uncertainties

How many of us talk ourselves out of investing or starting a business venture because there's so much we don't know? It is no coincidence that the largest number of reasons cited by reluctant investors from the earlier referenced joint study fell into this category when viewed beyond symptoms through to their underlying causes.

Both clarity of goal and accurate risk assessment (based on honest assessment of where you fall on the optimism-pessimism spectrum) can help you make an informed first step—but they're not enough. We also have to know *how* to respond to those risks, which largely depends on how well we deal with uncertainties.

First of all, uncertainty and risk are not the same thing. *Risk* is when the probabilities of future events can be estimated. Although risk is not defined as such, the average investor tends to view it as the potential for investment loss. *Uncertainty*, on the other hand, has to do with *not* knowing the odds of possible outcomes.

But let's cut through all the terminologies and define these terms so that we can all understand and apply them. We can simply define risk as how much we can lose in an investment or in a business venture. We can further quantify this term by simply saying that an investment with a very high level of risk can lead to our losing a bulk or the whole amount that we've invested.

On the other hand, uncertainty can be defined as the likelihood of something happening that could affect the outcome of the investment that we made into a portfolio or a business venture. Again, we can focus on just the downside since most of us don't go into panic mode if our investments make a handsome return. More importantly, we need to understand how we respond to these downside events should they occur. If a major recession hit, will we be able to afford losing all of our investments or a part of it, depending on how much risk was taken, and still pay for our necessities?

I hold the view that it is this inability to deal with uncertainties, along with having unclear goals and assigning the wrong level of risk, that keeps most of us from taking that first step. From my observations and personal experience, I've come down to three areas that, in my opinion, affect the way we deal with financial uncertainties—

1. Our level and areas of interest in investing or running a business
2. Our level of financial resilience
3. Our access to financial resources

LEVEL AND AREAS OF INTEREST

I suggest we start with those things we're most interested in. After all, action follows interest. If you have zero interest in investing or starting and operating a business venture, it is unlikely you will make the time or effort needed to research a potential investment portfolio, let alone put in the long hours needed to conceive, vet, develop, and execute a new business venture. When interest level is low, people tend to cut corners, make assumptions, and respond to difficulties more through reactive emotions than informed logic. This compounds the built-in uncertainties related to both investing and running a business, which leads to all kinds of bad decision-making (like knee-jerk selling the moment the market dips considerably).

In addition to the interest *level*, it helps to understand which aspects of investing or entrepreneurship interest us the most. For example, I'm a big-picture, systems-focused person energized by analyzing problems and coming up with novel solutions and strategies. In theory, this strength, combined with my experience in finance, could certainly lend itself to investing (analyzing companies that similarly innovate solutions to problems, for example). However, when I examined why I hesitated to fully invest my portfolio in the past, I realized that, while I do enjoy researching real estate (something that I can see and touch), I don't have the same level of interest needed in reading through company financial statements when evaluating stocks or bonds.

When launching my Chinese vocabulary app business, I felt motivated to help my children with their Chinese language class—especially my son, who was failing this course at the time. However, it was my genuine interest in finding a solution to this complex issue that provided a tremendous tailwind to keep me going through numerous challenges.

When it came to implementing the plan, I knew I had to account for my lack of interest in administrative tasks and certain other roles. So I got help from trusted contacts. One was a partner who helped me navigate the administrative aspects of incorporating a firm and managing the app development process. I also contracted with two consultants, one for technical issues and one for website development. Having this support helped me focus more fully on what truly interested me:

dealing with the strategic issues and resolving problems we encountered along the way.

Had I tried to single-handedly research and execute all aspects of this project—everything from securing the domain name for our website to learning technical minutiae about app coding—I never would have gotten my company off the ground.

Keep in mind that we don't need to have all the traits or skills to be successful investors and entrepreneurs. For example, some people cite the need for creativity among founders—but you don't *have* to be deeply creative to start a business. What you do need is honest self-assessment, coupled with business partners who embody those traits or skills you lack. A highly creative partner will likely appreciate someone more exacting and process minded.

Similarly, I have no issue doing the legwork to find an attractive investment opportunity—as long as it's related to real estate. However, if you ask me to do the same with a stock and bond portfolio, I would rely heavily on a financial advisor for support. By understanding where my interests lie, I can avoid the pitfalls of inaction.

In other words, when you're learning to navigate the uncertainties of investing or starting a business, your areas and levels of interest can help guide your hand in building your own unique Financial Independence Mindset—one that actually works for you and greatly increases your chances of taking that first step.

LEVEL OF FINANCIAL RESILIENCE

After figuring out which aspects of investing and/or entrepreneurship interested me (and which required outside support), I also needed to anticipate how I'd react to inevitable losses and other challenges. Knowing where I fall on the optimism-pessimism spectrum provides just part of the story. When things do go badly, how do I know how long I can hold out despite the level of risk in my portfolio or business venture?

In other words, how financially resilient am I?

Resilience is broadly defined by Oxford Languages as "the capacity to withstand or recover quickly from difficulties." According to the National Institutes of Health, *financial* resilience "relates to individuals' ability in coping with financial shock or recovering from financial difficulties."[2]

How do we assess financial resilience? To me, it comes down to one simple question: "How well could I sleep if I were to lose my job (stable income) or incur a large financial loss in my business venture or investment portfolio?" The ability to sleep soundly while going through a personal financial crisis demonstrates a high level of financial resilience. In contrast, those with lower financial resilience will tend to stay up all night ruminating on losses and all the ways things could get worse.

For example, when my niece just started her first job after graduating college, she called me to ask my opinion about investing in her first rental property in the US. I advised her to carefully consider the location and pricing of the unit, but, more importantly, to ensure she could still pay the mortgage should she lose her job (and/or fail to find a tenant), then her main source of income. Regardless of her risk tolerance, insufficient access to financial resources could spell disaster should things go wrong. In other words, whether she'll be able to sleep well without any safety nets when faced with financial challenges.

Since my niece at the time resided in Hong Kong, the fact that she could rely on her mom to provide financial support helped give her confidence to proceed. Besides, if the financial situation got dire enough, I could provide a second line of defense. At the time she was considering this investment, she still lived rent-free with her mother and had no other financial obligations. All of these factors boosted her financial resilience enough to allow such a large investment for her age.

Since there's a clear relationship between financial resilience and risk tolerance, those of us with lower financial resilience should take that into account when determining the amount of risk we're willing to take. That said, and as demonstrated by the example of my niece, there's one major factor that I believe helps determine our level of financial resilience even more than risk tolerance, and that is access to financial resources.

ACCESS TO FINANCIAL RESOURCES

Unlike risk tolerance, which seems tied to more fixed personality traits like optimism, access to financial resources can vary greatly throughout the course of our lives, often in ways we can directly control.

When we're still young, before we have kids of our own, many of us can temporarily move back home with our parents to save money, or even couch surf with friends, if needed. We can also avoid spending lavishly or falling into the trappings of lifestyle creep. All of these actions will help us to directly build up our financial resources.

After those early years in Hong Kong, I learned to avoid many of the trappings of lifestyle creep and maintained that discipline throughout my decades-long career. This helped me to build up my financial resources—despite my lack of a financial safety net like the one my niece enjoyed.

One of my rules that I adhered to over the last two-plus decades is to avoid spending beyond my salary. This means that whatever annual bonus I receive is simply that: a bonus. This discipline allowed me to save and invest for rainy days, while shortening the time it took to close my Passion Gap. It also allowed me to teach my children a key lesson about resource management through modeling good habits.

Beyond family, we can also develop professional and personal relationships to help fund our ventures. After all, top-rated MBA programs constantly advertise the great networks their schools provide, and for good reason.

Whether through networking, family support, or good money management, in learning to increase and optimize our financial resources, we can do a lot to strengthen our financial resilience (and, hopefully, sleep better at night).

FINANCIAL INDEPENDENCE MINDSET			
Step 1	Adopting Mindset of Multiple Sources of Income		
	✓ Employee		
	✓ Investor		
	✓ Entrepreneur/Contractor		
Step 2	Overcoming Barriers to Taking the First Step		
	Clarity of Goal	Assessment of Risk Level	Dealing with Uncertainties
	Who	Optimist	Interest
	Why	Pessimist	Financial Resiliency
	What		Access to Financial Resources
	How Much		
	When		

What I've learned from my personal experience and research is that while adopting the Investor and Entrepreneur Mindsets is necessary, it is not sufficient. We also need to understand our individual circumstances, traits, and goals in order to put our plans into action and overcome the obstacles to taking that first step.

PUTTING CONCEPTS INTO PRACTICE

When I launched my side business, I was in my mid-50s with two young children to support. My financial goal was beyond modest: to break even in terms of annual operating costs. That's because my key motivator for starting the business was to help both my children (and their cohorts facing similar challenges) to pass their Chinese exams.

Plus, I had already begun writing this book, and I realized that starting a business of my own would help me to better develop, apply, and verify the concepts presented in this chapter and elsewhere. After all, I needed to "walk the walk" and not just "talk the talk."

Before diving in, I took the time to self-analyze. Given my naturally more pessimistic outlook, I took on little risk with my business venture. It is no coincidence that my investment portfolio is also constructed relatively conservatively.

As a result of my high level of interest, I personally researched and built my own real estate portfolio. This is in contrast to relying heavily on a financial advisor to help put together my investment portfolio. With a good understanding of my areas of interest, I left certain roles to others and focused on those I knew I had both the skills and motivation to follow through on. Because of my greater access to financial resources, my financial resilience was much higher when I took on this business venture or in my investment portfolio, compared to even ten years ago, let alone early in my career (when I struggled to pay for my living expenses). All of this helps to nudge my outlook toward greater optimism, which will allow me to pursue higher risk opportunities moving forward (rather than only seeing the downsides involved).

Earlier in this chapter, I suggested that where we land on the optimism-pessimism spectrum tends to remain at least somewhat fixed as a personality trait. I say "somewhat" because I do believe that increasing our access to financial resources can significantly improve our financial resilience. This higher level of financial resiliency will, in turn, increase our optimism, leading us to be able to take on more risk when investing or running a business. I view this as a built-in mechanism for adjusting our risk level. Plus, we can exercise more direct control over access to financial resources by spending less, saving more, and/or building relationships with those who can help provide support.

Looking back, I certainly wish I'd chosen differently on the banks of the Huangpu River those many years ago. After all, I was young and single, with enough access to resources to buffer my financial resiliency. I also had sufficient interest to do the necessary research. Knowing what I know today, I would say that the factors preventing me from acting on that investment opportunity were insufficient clarity of goal, lack of self-awareness (especially about my pessimism), and not having a thorough understanding of how I dealt with uncertainties.

I learned that I don't have to be a wealthy optimist with a deep interest in either investing or entrepreneurship, as frequently touted. Instead, I can customize my unique approach to taking that first step in order to achieve the Financial Independence Mindset that works for me.

TAKEAWAYS

Financial independence isn't just for the independently wealthy. It also isn't about amassing enough money to never have to work again. Instead, it has more to do with mindset. Specifically, building the self-awareness, skills, and belief to know that, no matter what happens, you'll always be able to financially provide for yourself and your family.

It's not just the Warren Buffetts and Elon Musks of the world who can benefit from the Entrepreneur and Investor Mindsets. As we move toward a more uncertain future global job market led by the 4th-IR, any professional in any role can benefit from identifying and solving problems, as well as building investment portfolios beyond employee-defined contribution programs.

I certainly don't advocate that we all avoid or quit traditional employment. Not everyone has the temperament/drive, financial goals, risk tolerance, or ability to deal with uncertainties needed to become a major investor or start-up founder. However, even for those who choose to work for someone else, I encourage exploring ways to both apply the more dynamic, problem-solving "true" Entrepreneur Mindset to their work and to supplement their salaries with contract gigs and investment options.

Beyond developing the Investor and Entrepreneur Mindsets, we need to also overcome obstacles preventing us from taking action. First, that means getting clear on goals. This clarity will help us stay the course for whatever challenges life throws at us.

Next, we need to assess our risk tolerance. Understanding where we lie on the optimism-pessimism spectrum will help ensure that we employ the appropriate level of risk over the long term.

To better deal with financial uncertainties, we need to understand our areas and levels of interest. This helps determine where to depend on ourselves and where to seek a partner and/or financial advisor. Finally, our access to financial resources will help us recover when facing setbacks along the way (and help us sleep soundly).

There's nothing wrong with starting small. As long as you make an informed *first step*, your investing or entrepreneurial journey can help build your self-belief over time through small, incremental wins that boost your resilience, increasing your ability to accommodate more risk (as you become more optimistic), and your chances of success.

In tomorrow's workplace, I believe this requires taking those first steps needed toward developing a true Financial Independence Mindset.

In doing so, we can free ourselves up to focus on what truly brings long-term happiness. As we'll see next, it can also help us discover our life's passions and cultivate greater meaning and purpose for ourselves and others. The final section of this book pulls together what we covered in Parts 1 and 2, while connecting it all to matters of passion, meaning, and purpose.

> **LEARNING POINTS**
>
> - A *Financial Independence Mindset* is not about accumulating a certain amount of money, but rather developing the belief that no matter the circumstances, you'll always be able to provide financially for yourself and your loved ones.
>
> - Based on your unique attributes, you can develop your own combination of working for others, working for yourself, and investing.
>
> - Those raised and educated within the Employee Mindset will likely face obstacles when taking the first step toward investing and/or running a business.
>
> - With the clarity of goal and self-awareness, even underprivileged and/or risk-averse individuals can learn to better deal with *uncertainties*, increase their *access to resources*, and build both *financial resilience* and *income security*.

SELF-REFLECTION

- What did financial independence mean to you before and after reading this chapter? Has your view changed, and how?

- Do you believe you're able to earn income from investments and entrepreneurship, with or without traditional employment? What proportion of each income source best suits your current financial mindset? What proportion of each income source would you like to ultimately achieve?

PART 3
INTEGRATION

7

DEFINING AND FINDING PASSION

It is obvious that we can no more explain a passion to a person
who has never experienced it than we can explain light to the blind.

—T. S. Eliot

"Papa, do you think I can play in the NBA when I grow up?"

I looked down at E's hopeful face—from my own unimpressive height of five feet, ten inches—and smiled. As a young teenager, I used to hit the basketball courts every chance I got. Before class, at lunchtime, immediately after school, and on weekends. Still, I'd known not to get my hopes up about making my high school team.

Despite my love for the game, I simply wasn't athletically gifted enough to overcome my height disadvantage. Nor did I have the intensity of drive compared to my classmates and others I played with. Besides, our school players were *good*. During my freshman year, our high school team—which in fact did produce an NBA starter—had won the state championship.

Decades later, here was my ten-year-old son, asking my opinion on his budding dream. Granted, this would prove to be a passing impulse. At the time, he'd only done a few Saturday morning classes at one of Singapore's international schools—skills and drills followed by a 15-minute full-court game with his newly acquainted teammates. But at that moment, he radiated a child's pure, unadulterated passion for the game.

Bear in mind that E's mother barely breaks five-one, and despite the outliers—NBA point guard Muggsy Bogues was only five-three and his fellow pro Spud Webb, who famously won an all-star Slam Dunk contest, was five-six—the average height for NBA players today tends to stand at around six-six. But even if we were a family of giants, what were the odds of E ever ranking among the 450 players in the world's most elite basketball league?

How do we, as parents, teach our children to be realistic about their passions (fleeting though they may be) without discouraging them from pursuing their interests? Sure, most kids won't grow up to become a professional athlete, film actor, or even a successful social media influencer or paid video gamer. But does that mean they shouldn't try?

At some point or another, most parents get confronted with their child's NBA dreams, art major, or another youthful passion. How do we help our children grasp the difference between possibility and probability without killing their ability to joyfully create, to train hard, or to dream big? Should we urge them to shelve these goals for something more practical or tell them to shoot for the moon? After all, the late Steve Jobs famously said, "The only way to do great work is to love what you do," and he founded one of the world's most valuable companies.

As you can probably guess, I hesitate to toss passion completely out of the work equation. But, given our understanding of jobs (and other income sources) as mainly a means to the end of serving our North Star values—is pursuing passion truly the "only way to do great work," as Jobs put it?

Let's dive into how passion fits into the equation of our professional and personal lives.

WORLDLY ADVICE

Like Steve Jobs, Warren Buffett regularly advises young people in America to pursue work they love. In the 2022 annual letter to Berkshire Hathaway shareholders, Buffett noted that he'd "urged that they [university students] seek employment in (1) the field and (2) with the kind of people they would select if they had no need for money."[1] Buffett also said in a 2019 interview with *Inc.*, "Why do I get up every day and jump out of bed and I'm excited at 88? It's because I love what I do and love the people I do it with."[2]

The rationale is simple: If you do what you're passionate about, you'll work hard and therefore excel. Hard work and excellence in turn lead to success in that field, and the money will follow. Many eminently successful entrepreneurs, celebrities, athletes, and entertainers—not to mention, a growing number of social media influencers, life coaches, and motivational speakers—swear by this argument.

Take for example Simon Sinek, an American author and inspirational speaker, who, at the time of this book's publication, boasted three million Instagram followers and over eight million LinkedIn followers. According to Sinek, "working hard for something we don't care about is called stress; working hard for something we love is called passion."³

Even as far back as the fifth and sixth centuries BCE, the Chinese philosopher Confucius advised followers to "choose a job you love, and you will never have to work a day in your life."

What If Passion Just Isn't Enough?

What if my son devotes his youth to nothing but practicing basketball, only to find himself in a professional dead end with no other marketable skills and a pile of debt and regrets? This might have been the fate of billionaire investor Mark Cuban, who also dreamed of playing professional basketball as a kid.

As Cuban shared on Amazon's *Insights for Entrepreneurs* series, "I used to be passionate about being a professional basketball player. Then I realized I had a seven-inch vertical."⁴ Cuban tried baseball next, but his inability to throw a fastball dampened his Major League dreams. So he moved on from youthful aspirations, pursued a business degree, and eventually became a successful entrepreneur and investor, which led him to become a "shark" on the popular television series *Shark Tank*. He is also a minority owner of the Dallas Mavericks NBA team.

When it comes to the passion vs. money question, Cuban doesn't pull any punches. He thinks that telling young people to follow their passion perpetuates "one of life's greatest lies." Instead, he advises young people to put effort into things that they are good at.

Mike Rowe, former host of the Discovery Channel's *Dirty Jobs*, suggests following opportunities. Rowe travels the US apprenticing for, well, *dirty jobs*—the kind no child dreams about in primary school: ostrich wrangler, bat guano harvester, septic tank cleaner, and so on.

In a 2018 CNBC interview, Rowe said, "I met countless people who were doing things that . . . looked like the thing you would go out of your way to avoid. But then, when you sit down and talk to them, you find out that they make six figures a year, and they have a vacation, and they have enough balance in their life to coach their kid's little league team, and they don't have any debt."[5] In other words, while passion may not factor much into their workday, these professionals typically have enough time, money, and energy left over to pursue what they love outside of work.

Google "passion vs. money" and you'll find a lot of practical voices like these. Many, such as Rowe and Cuban, point out that not all passions are profitable. Others argue that the quickest way to lose your passion is to do it for work, reducing something you fiercely love to budgets, negotiations, and other transactional buzzkills. Finally, what if your passion changes or you lack the discipline or drive to compete?

Much like our earlier attempt to find a universal definition for "happiness," these questions produce endless debates and polarizing responses. So, I decided to leave the maze of Google search results and talk to successful professionals I know and respect.

Adam Khoo, for example, is a well-known Singaporean author, entrepreneur, motivational speaker, and trainer who founded Adam Khoo Wealth Academy and Adam Khoo Learning Technologies, becoming a millionaire by his late twenties. Khoo and I spent over an hour in his unassuming office, nestled in an industrial area in eastern Singapore.

During our talk, I was not surprised to hear Khoo enthusiastically promote passion as a necessary ingredient for great success. "If you don't love what you do, you'll never make it big," he said. "I can't imagine myself working a day on something I don't enjoy. Not even for two minutes."

As we spoke further, I learned more about his upbringing. Khoo freely admitted that he was fortunate to grow up in relatively affluent surroundings. His father had founded a successful Singapore-based advertising agency and his mother worked as a lifestyle editor at a leading local publishing firm.

For the sake of comparison, I shared how I'd always relied on myself: to buy anything that wasn't handed down, to save up for a car, and to pay off all my school loans, as well as rent and all living expenses as a young adult. Khoo acknowledged that, unlike in the US, most young adults in Singapore continue to live in their parents' homes after college—often until they get married. In contrast, most young Americans are expected to promptly move out on their own upon graduating from college or getting their first "real job."

As we said our goodbyes, Khoo said, "I guess there is no right or wrong answer." Once again, we find that the definition of "good advice" depends on who's asking it. In other words, discerning the difference between good and bad advice involves understanding whether and how it applies to you and your unique circumstances (assuming you know what your passion is in the first place).

WHAT EVEN IS PASSION?

Speaking of definitions, let's back up and examine what exactly we're talking about when we talk about "passion vs. money." In a previous chapter, we looked at practical considerations surrounding money—particularly, *how much is enough?*

Next, let's figure out what exactly we mean by "passion"—and how it fits into the equation when considering what work to pursue.

All or Nothing?

If we stick to a generic, nonreligious, and nonsexual context, Dictionary.com defines "passion" as "any powerful or compelling emotion or feeling, as love or hate." However, for our purposes (thinking about passion in regards to career paths), the *Britannica* dictionary offers a better description: "a strong feeling of enthusiasm or excitement for something or about doing something."

Sounds reasonable enough—but then I stumbled upon a 2010 self-help book, *Aspire*, by Kevin Hall. An author, business consultant, speaker, and coach, Hall dedicated a chapter to "passion," where he defined it to mean something we love for which we're willing to make sacrifices. I find this definition to be quite applicable to our discussion. After all, when pursuing a career path, we often make sacrifices, in terms of what we love or how we live, and when individuals follow passion, they tend to face much higher risk—unless they are highly gifted in their field of passion that falls into a well-compensated role or industry.

Based on descriptions from these and others—authors, friends, experts, job recruiters, and, of course, people with opinions on the internet—it seems to me that most people use the word to describe *extreme interest*, not just in learning and knowing a lot about something, but also in *doing* something about it. However, is it fair to leave out sacrifices that may need to be made in pursuit of passion?

When thinking about how to define "passion," I began to ask several other questions of my own: Does everyone have a passion? If not, does the passion vs. money question have any meaning for them? Alternatively, is it possible that we *all* have passions, if to varying degrees of intensity?

Taking myself as an example, I could argue that I possess passion, at least to some degree, since I'm at my computer early this Sunday morning—and just about anytime I have spare time—working on this book. But would I die if I didn't sit down and type out my thoughts on a Sunday morning? Certainly not. While I deeply love thinking about and writing this book, I would easily stop right now and never look back if it seriously threatened my material security—let alone my ability to literally *survive*. I may choose to spend my spare time doing this thing, but I have never neglected priorities like spending quality time with my children or fulfilling work obligations in order to write.

Does that mean I lack sufficient passion? Or that I simply "chose money" over passion?

Frankly, I'm not satisfied with either conclusion (and not just because I'd have a shorter and less interesting book that way). I suspect that, just as we're all motivated by different constellations of North Star values and comfortable with different lifestyle levels, we all experience varying degrees of passion. With this in mind, I've come up with a two-part definition of passion that applies to my circumstances.

Traits as Well as Roles

When most people talk about passion and work, they often speak in terms of specific jobs. How do you most passionately pursue sports? You become a pro athlete. Meanwhile, those passionate about engineering become engineers. Similarly, art equals artists, and teaching equals teachers. Right?

Sure—sometimes—but that's just part of the story. Next, consider a person's primary North Star and lifestyle level, then determine whether pursuing that NBA dream or art history major aligns with their required budget and primary core value (most often Serving Family).

I think a lot of us weigh these things already, consciously or not. That would explain why so many warn against pursuing only passion when making career choices. They know that most of us are not likely to break into professional sports or earn enough as, say, a painter or sculptor. Even the field of education tends to pay far below what many would need to sustain their lifestyle.

But what if we looked at this differently? Instead of just focusing on the most traditional career applications—athlete, engineer, artist, teacher—why not also examine transferable skills, proficiencies, and attributes?

In other words, not just roles but also their traits.

As I see it, someone can have a passion for understanding and solving complex technical problems (STEM traits), creating and sharing aesthetically appealing things (artistic traits), imparting knowledge to others (pedagogical traits), and so on. With it viewed this way, we can identify the strengths and characteristics of our particular passions, then figure out how we can apply those within any number of professional roles and fields.

For example, I enjoy imparting knowledge to others—but that doesn't mean I can't "follow my passion" unless I teach students in a traditional classroom. Instead, I can use these same traits to become an author, consultant, life coach, or even a team leader within a company.

When talking to people who initially couldn't tell me what their passion was, I tried redefining the word in these terms—and it didn't take long to see that most know what they most deeply enjoy. I can relate. I had the same issue when trying to pin down my "passion." As a kid, I (like E) might have said basketball. In college, I suspected it might be psychology. More recently, I've found that I really love teaching. Fast-forward a few decades and I'm not a baller, a psychologist, or a school teacher. I used to think I'd outgrown my passions or maybe just kept them at arm's length, relegated to ordinary "interest" status.

REDEFINING PASSION

ROLES	TRAITS
STEM	Understanding and solving complex technical problems
PSYCHOLOGY/ SOCIOLOGY	Understanding and solving complex societal and people issues
ARTS	Creating beautiful or appealing things (audio, visual, written)
MEDICINE	Understanding and solving complex biological issues
TEACHING	Imparting knowledge to others
SPORTS	Engaging and excelling in activities that align mind and body
SERVICE	Creating positive emotional experiences for others
CIVICS	Solving complex legal and governance issues

However, when viewed as personal and professional traits, I can easily identify that I'm passionate about both understanding and solving complex people-related issues and imparting knowledge to others. I can also see that it's possible to apply these passions to many professional roles outside of psychology and education. In fact, I've already done so in different ways during my decades-long career in financial services. I just mostly didn't realize it at the time.

Range of Intensity

The second part of my (re)definition of "passion" acknowledges that each person feels different *degrees* of intensity toward whatever it is they enjoy doing. I've noticed that we tend to only apply the word "passion" to extreme examples, such as famous artists, professional athletes, and even martyrs. We call to mind people like Van Gogh spending his dwindling cash on paint instead of food or rent, ultramarathon runners and decathletes, or even the anti-Nazi dissident pastor Bonhoeffer, who gave his life for his cause.

If that's the only measure of "real" passion, most of us won't even come close.

What about those of us who feel drawn by their passions, but only to a point? If we aren't willing to sacrifice life and limb for our interest, should that disqualify us? Instead of categorizing these individuals—including myself—as passionless grunts and suits, why not honor the full spectrum of intensity levels when it comes to areas of interest? In other words, let's explore passion as a continuum, reflecting at one end an avid hobby, and at the other extreme the Van Goghs and Bonhoeffers of the world. In between, we find a range of intensity levels, plus the traits that go along with each.

It's my view that everyone has a passion (likely more than one). Of course, some people really do go on to become the "fortunate few" who fulfill their childhood dream of becoming a professional athlete or artist. Others go straight to a more traditional path like engineering or education.

Still others, like me, may only recognize their passions when defined by intensity (not heroic, perhaps, but strong enough!), as well as personal/professional interests (i.e. traits), rather than specific jobs or roles.

FINDING MY PASSION

Hopefully you now have a better understanding of the traits and intensity level of your interests. If, like me, you're a more pragmatic professional—someone who's taken a position mainly (or purely) as a means to an end—these passions may not appear to carry much weight in your daily existence. It can be difficult to even imagine incorporating more excitement, focus, and flavor into a professional world. I've certainly been there.

I've also learned that, although we may not be able to instantly transform our professional lives into something more inspiring on all fronts, we can achieve this at some point in time. In the meantime, we can change both our perspective and our approach to infuse more passion into our work.

For example, after accepting a job offer in 2001 from my former boss and moving to Singapore, I'd hoped to find professional fulfillment working for a leader and company who shared my values. Months later, I still felt uninspired and frustrated. I may have appreciated my boss, but a misalignment remained: between my deep interest in understanding human psychology and educating people on one hand, and the more profit-driven realities of an investment management sales role on the other.

Even within that setting, by expanding my definition of passion to centralize traits over roles and acknowledging where I fell on the spectrum of intensity, I managed to align my passions with my career in the investment management industry. First, I acknowledged the value of my traits: understanding and solving complex people problems (psychology) and imparting knowledge to others (teaching). Then I assessed my intensity level, placing it at around a seven or eight out of ten—not high enough to impact my family's stability by abandoning finance to become a social worker or school teacher—but enough to make me unhappy at work. Then, I set out to solve my own complex people problem: I began researching how to better apply those traits within my current field.

I homed in on a problem related to lack of client interest or engagement in their own 401(k)s. You may recall from Chapter 4 that in the 1980s, retirement plans shifted to 401(k)s and other DC plans (based on tax-deferred employee contributions). Previously, workers could rely on DB plans, under which employers took on the sole responsibility of providing lifetime income to retirees and their dependents.

While the previous DB plans were managed by highly trained pension fund departments, the nature of the newer DC plans, like 401(k)s, meant that employees themselves were now responsible for making investment decisions that determined their ability to retire. However, a number of people who contribute to a 401(k) rarely check in on their portfolios—let alone actively manage and reinvest (rebalance) their holdings.

To learn more, I read a joint survey conducted by my then-firm and an outside consultant. It categorized investors into three groups, based on their levels of knowledge, interest, and time (KIT) when dealing with investment matters. Unsurprisingly, they determined that the group with the lowest KIT scores were the least likely to respond to investment information or engage consistently with their retirement portfolios—despite how much they needed information and support. This group of low-KIT individuals also formed the majority of survey participants.

To find solutions to this problem, I began researching a product offered by my then-company to US-based DC plan participants. Today, these products are commonly known as *target date funds*. This product offers a managed, diversified fund of different asset classes (based on an investor's relative proximity to retirement or another time-based goal), which takes the onus off of low-KIT investors. I ended up introducing a target date fund to a local bank-owned asset management firm in 2002—and, in so doing, became the first financial professional to bring target date funds customized for the local investor needs into Singapore's financial markets.

Next, I created training programs to help regional institutional investors construct portfolios in a more efficient way, based on sophisticated models developed by my colleagues at my then-firm. This made me one of the early professionals in the investment management industry to carry out a consultative approach to selling in the region, a model that has served me, my clients, and my employers since the early 2000s.

By understanding and redirecting my passion-related traits, I've managed to nurture my passions and achieve greater success in my career.

More recently, I went on to apply my transferable passions to areas outside of my day job through both writing this book and creating the Chinese vocabulary app to help my children succeed at school.

As with our values, goals, and lifestyle preferences, passion is a deeply subjective matter. Again, be wary of taking advice from those who may not share your degree of passion or understand how you can apply the unique traits (e.g., skills, aptitudes, etc.) associated with you and your interests. I believe that we can all find ways to utilize our passion(s) both within and outside of our work. Above all, we just need self-reflection to understand both our interest levels and the transferable traits of our passions—plus some creative thinking. Referencing the previous examples of how I translated my "passion" into "traits" (that I was able to further utilize in my role at work), try doing the same exercise to see if you're able to derive your traits from your passion, or the other way around.

When faced with E's question about becoming an NBA player, I didn't resort to some platitude, such as, "You can be anything you put your mind to." Neither did I advise him to give up on his passion altogether. Instead, we sat down together to work out the probabilities of his ever ranking among the top 450 basketball players in the world. First, I showed him that there are more than 20,000 high schools just in the US alone. So if each of these 20,000-plus high school teams had 12 players, he'd be competing with more than 240,000 other players—just to get one of about 34,000 spots available within university basketball teams in the US. Finally, he'd have to compete with all of these college players (not counting players outside the US) to become one of 60 players drafted each year by the NBA.

E agreed that these were slim odds (to say the least), so we discussed other available options, like playing for a professional basketball team in Singapore. This route would pay much less than the NBA, of course, and either way, his basketball career would be limited to just a few years—maybe a decade at best. After that, he'd likely become a school basketball coach.

We went on to discuss how his love for basketball can be understood in terms of the common associated traits. For example, if E had continued developing his passion for basketball, he would have developed skills and attributes related to competitive drive, strategic thinking, and teamwork—all of which he could transfer to other professions.

At the end, I told E that if he still wanted to pursue a professional basketball career, he'd be wise to generate income from an investment portfolio, or start a side business, to help him afford his preferred lifestyle while pursuing basketball and coaching here in Singapore. If he managed to break into professional basketball within the less lucrative context of Singapore, income generated from investments or business venture could potentially allow him to bridge his Passion Gap—pursuing what he loves while earning what he wants, with the help of a diversified portfolio of income sources that support both his lifestyle level and his North Stars.

TAKEAWAYS

How do we, as parents, navigate this rift of uncertainty between passion and money? Should we or our children spend these brief lives courageously pursuing what we love most at work? Or should we wise up and focus on earning to avoid financial struggles and disappointments? Finally, why are these arguments often so binary?

I don't subscribe to the "all or nothing" mentality surrounding pursuing one's passion professionally. I don't think we can claim passion in life only if we're willing to suffer huge sacrifices in service to that passion. Like most parents, I don't want my children to struggle financially in order to do what they love. You can bet I won't encourage either of them to consider the kind of work featured on Mike Rowe's Discovery Channel show, *Dirty Jobs* (unless, I suppose, they develop a passion for harvesting bat guano or wrangling ostriches). I especially don't want them to pursue their interests if doing so places them in extreme hardship—unless their primary North Stars somehow direct them toward this less trodden path (in that case, I probably can't do much to stop them).

While I remain realistic about, for example, the chances of my son growing up to become a global basketball star, I'd still prefer that both he and my daughter, S, build careers they deeply enjoy, rather than enduring some miserable 40-hour workweek just to pay the bills.

That's why I define passion to include not only jobs or roles but also their associated traits. By this definition, I argue that everyone has a passion (or more than one).

Further, I see passion as a spectrum. Some people may never experience intense devotion for their main interests, and others may indeed be willing to give up everything else to pursue what lights them up. Most of us, I believe, fall somewhere in between these two extremes. But wherever one's passion lies on this continuum, I believe passion should factor into anyone's career planning, at least to some degree. When you're deciding what professional route to take, it's important to factor in your transferable passion-related *traits* and also consider the level of intensity you feel regarding your passion. This, in addition to practical matters related to income and lifestyle, as well as the all-important North Stars, can help you decide to what extent passion should factor into your early career planning.

This also sets us up to finally tackle the principle theme of this book: the concept of the "Passion Gap." This idea describes the reality that, while everyone has at least one deep interest that lights them up, not everyone can pursue that passion wholesale as their career—at least, not right away. And while not everyone can turn their passion into the centerpiece of their professional lives immediately, I believe that, with the correct understanding and strategic planning, everyone can and should incorporate more and more of what they love into their lives throughout the course of their lives, including at work.

LEARNING POINTS

- Passion does not have to be an "all or nothing" pursuit.

- Everyone has particular *interests*, although the intensity levels of these interests greatly differ from one individual to the next.

- For most of us, pursuing passion through work has more to do with incorporating related *traits* and their levels of intensity.

- In this way, anyone can integrate their passions into their professional lives, without having to directly chase specific and unrealistic childhood dream roles.

SELF-REFLECTION

- What are your greatest interests and levels of intensity for each?

- What are some transferable skills, proficiencies, and attributes associated with these interests?

8

BRIDGING THE PASSION GAP

It's not about the money. It's about the lifestyle of earning more, thinking more, learning more, and becoming more.

—Mark Cuban[1]

"What are your plans going forward?" my former boss said as we sat down to dinner on the last day of a business trip to Australia. We were discussing my departure from the company that I joined more than a decade ago. I replied that I didn't have any concrete plans other than to spend more time with E and S and continue to work on my book.

Unlike previous periods when I was left without a job and the stable income that accompanied it, I didn't panic. In fact, I mainly felt relief.

For about four years before this conversation, I'd been preparing for such an outcome (and secretly hoping for it for at least two years as the frequency of work-related travel had returned). I'd dearly missed spending time with my children since my divorce. Every other weekend simply wasn't enough, and I felt the internal emptiness that accompanies straying from my primary North Star.

In short, I knew I could now maintain my family's lifestyle without this position. Previously, I'd even considered resigning, but I couldn't shake the notion that such a move would have been irresponsible. The money that I would leave on the table was just too good—not to mention well earned, having dedicated more than 12 years to this company. I had resolved to stay the course, accumulating as much as I could for the sake of the kids' financial security while developing and pursuing interests outside of work.

As I left that fateful business dinner, I realized how relatively easy it was to now walk away from this job. I already had side projects to focus my newfound time and energy into: a Chinese language app I'd developed and could now either expand or sell, and a passion project—writing this book—well underway.

My mind began swimming with new possibilities. I could always return to a traditional job in my field—or I could lean into writing, consulting, teaching, conducting workshops, and/or serving my community more through volunteer work. Above all, I wanted to spend more time with my two children as they moved toward and into their teen years. With this last thought, it occurred to me that I now have what my friend Mike had enjoyed: the luxury of free time to spend serving my North Stars and directly pursuing my passions.

Despite a costly divorce and other curveballs, I could now support my lifestyle while applying my interests *directly* to what matters most to me. In other words, I had bridged my own Passion Gap.

Now, let's address that question of timing—and, more to the point, how to speed up the journey to bridging our Passion Gap.

ASKING THE WRONG QUESTION

While investigating the intersection between passion and money, I've come to the conclusion that we're asking the wrong question. Instead of seeing the matter as some binary question that demands we choose between either passion or money, why not arrange our lives to support both? I happen to believe we can all get there. It just takes time and effort to reconcile the two, not to mention self-awareness, strategy, and patience.

Assuming there's often some trade-off between passion and money, let's review how we're defining these terms. In Chapter 7, we discussed "passion" through the lens of personal interests associated with different intensity levels and specific transferable traits we can identify, develop, and apply within a number of fields. As for "money," let's refer back to Chapter 3, which offers a method for self-identifying how much income each individual requires to support their preferred lifestyle level.

For those whose convictions to their passion of Serving God or Serving Society vastly outweighs their low lifestyle preferences, the choice doesn't require much in the way of contemplation. However, most of us prefer a higher standard of living in Serving Family. Meanwhile, many of us approach our passions with considerably less intensity. This combination of low-intensity passion and higher lifestyle requirements can make it harder to discover our passion and bridge that gap.

Even when we put aside those whose North Stars are Serving God or Serving Society, I realized that not everyone who Serves Family has a major gap to bridge when it comes to achieving both passion and money. Some youth athletes or actors get recruited by talent scouts even before their careers begin. Others inherit fortunes and can launch successful careers of their choosing right out of the gate. All of that said, I'd argue that these people represent a slim minority of people overall who can follow their passion from the get-go.

For most of us, bridging the Passion Gap takes time. Sometimes quite a bit of it. I've seen friends who spent three decades diligently working to close their Passion Gap, while others pull it off much quicker.

First, let's start with the exceptions—those lucky few who can simply pursue their passions from day one. I call them "Passion Now" people.

PASSION NOW PEOPLE

If you happen to be independently wealthy—or as a starving artist or someone choosing to live an extremely humble or ascetic lifestyle or a basketball prodigy—you're probably not too concerned about this passion vs. money question. However, if you're reading this book, I'll assume you at least want to make enough to comfortably support yourself and your family and provide them with opportunities.

Who are the Passion Now people—those lucky individuals who can launch directly into their professed passions within the professional realm? I believe that there are four such groups, which I'm calling trust fund kids, starving artists, down-to-earthers, and the fortunate few.

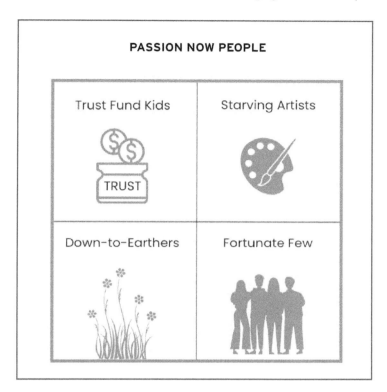

Trust Fund Kids

When we hear the label "trust fund kids," most of us instantly think of a particular high-profile individual who benefits from vast generational wealth. For me, it's Paris Hilton. If you Google her name, you'll find her described by Wikipedia as "an American media personality, socialite, businesswoman, model, singer, and actress." Hilton is the great-granddaughter of Conrad Hilton, the founder behind the Hilton Hotels and Resorts hospitality chain.

For Hilton, and those in similar circumstances, money is no consideration when selecting a career. A quick Google search uncovers several passions she's already pursued: entrepreneurship, acting, and singing. The idea of "success," as commonly defined in financial terms, is less relevant in her case. She's already able to pursue things for reasons other than income. Despite coming from a background of wealth, Hilton has stated that she's not like other trust fund kids as she chose to work for her own money.

Starving Artists

We all know or have heard of someone who falls into the category of "starving artists." Vincent van Gogh certainly comes to mind. The Dutch painter, born in 1853, is still regarded as one of the greatest painters to have ever lived. Although his art sells for record-breaking amounts today, this was not the case until well after his death.

Van Gogh would famously spend what little he had not on food, but on painting supplies—despite his paintings not selling at the time.

For a true starving artist like Van Gogh, such sacrifices simply don't register in the same way. These individuals will pursue their passions to the end, even if it means disregarding other aspects of life.

Down-to-Earthers

In Chapter 3, we explored the link between money and happiness along a range of lifestyle levels ($–$$$$$). People content to remain at the $ lifestyle (by choice, not necessity) represent the third camp of people who can safely pursue passion anytime. I refer to these individuals as down-to-earthers. These are those, somewhat rare, individuals who need exceedingly little in the way of material comforts in order to serve their North Star values and feel perfectly fulfilled.

I've noticed among down-to-earthers I know that most follow the primary North Star of either Serving God or Serving Society. One example is Pastor K, the father of my friend Samuel. Pastor K made sacrifices impacting not just his own material resources, but those of his family as well.

That said, it's possible for down-to-earthers to follow the primary North Star of Serving Family; they simply prioritize love and attention over material gains. They might spend all their family vacations camping out in a tent under the stars. Perhaps they see college as a luxury their children should find a way to fund on their own, either to learn the value of work and independence, or because they don't see higher education (and the higher incomes generally associated with it) as a prerequisite for a happy and meaningful life.

Overall, because of their modest $ lifestyle needs, down-to-earthers are often able to immediately follow their passions when seeking work, even when these career paths yield much less in terms of financial reward and upward mobility.

Fortunate Few

The final category of Passion Now people is what I call the "fortunate few." The common denominator is that they are not only highly passionate about what they do; they also tend to have the rare talent and motivation required to actually rise to the top echelons of their fields. And to boot, their field of work happens to pay a great deal of money.

Michael Jordan comes to mind. Individuals like him not only possess the unlikely potential to rise to reach the pinnacle of success within a lucrative and extremely competitive field like professional basketball in the world's most competitive league, but they also have the drive to compete with elite talent. In addition to sports and entertainment, the fortunate few include successful entrepreneurs and investors, especially within high-profile industries like finance and information technology.

While the fortunate few, and those who round up the Passion Now people, are indeed "fortunate," they account for a minority among us. The majority, those who I label as "Passion Gap" people, will be the subject of our next topic.

PASSION GAP PEOPLE

Most of us grow up with neither million-dollar trust funds nor one-in-a-million artistic or athletic talent. Plus, the majority of people aren't willing to sacrifice basic comforts for our passions. How do those of us in the majority weigh our passion and our lifestyle needs? I suggest we start with the definition of "fortunate few" from the earlier section.

Where most people stop at this definition, I argue for expanding beyond those passionate professionals performing at the very top of their fields and paid at the $$$$$ lifestyle level. I believe the even more modest earners can number among their ranks. For example, I would argue that my older brother, H, belongs in this category of the fortunate few. As a hardware engineer who leads a small team, H's not exceptionally well paid, compared even to his colleagues in software development, let alone a professional athlete. So how does he fit into the fortunate few? It has to do with proportionality. My brother is deeply interested in engineering and had known that he wanted to go into this line of work from a young age. He's sufficiently talented in his field of work to earn the level of income needed to provide for his relatively modest $$–$$$ lifestyle requirements, while serving his primary North Star (Serving Family).

After all, as discussed in Chapter 3, happiness cannot be measured simply by dollar signs, but instead in terms of an alignment of North Star values, financial values and aspirations, and—as we're now exploring—deep interests or passions. He may not be Michael Jordan, or even some tech "genius," but my brother, H, managed to sustainably align his passion, skill set, and pay early in his career, albeit within a much lower income bracket.

My brother's experience pursuing his passion within a more modest context offers an example of how the majority of us non-prodigies can also achieve the ranks of the fortunate few.

With this new, more accessible definition of the "fortunate few" in hand, we can now explore how ordinary people, like my brother H, can bridge their gap in the quickest possible time. After all, I suspect that most of us realistically aspire to the $$ to $$$ lifestyle—some middle ground between just getting by and extravagant wealth.

If we want to provide a somewhat modest lifestyle for ourselves and our families, why do the majority of us feel the need to give up on our passions and instead pursue money alone? Part of it comes down to the advice of parents, who (as Mark Cuban advised) frequently urge their children to pursue something practical, like law, business, or medicine, despite their lack of avid interest in these fields. Those parents, fearing the consequences of the 4th-IR, will likely urge their children toward

STEM subjects. Ultimately, these children will need to financially support themselves and their families.

I believe this reaction, though rational and well intended, feeds into the polarized view of passion vs. money, and can quickly lead our children to unhappy professional and personal lives. While I disagree with Steve Jobs's binary opinion that the "only way to do great work is to love what you do," intuition tells me that having at least some level of passion (defined as an avid interest you've developed, along with transferable traits that come along with that) is a major predictor for achieving both professional success and a deeper sense of fulfillment from your work.

Why? Because without passion or interest, it would be extremely difficult for most of us to dedicate the amount of time needed to develop the deep level of knowledge and skills (i.e., traits) needed to attain the expertise—in any given field—especially if you'd like to support a higher lifestyle level.

I'm basing this partly on the idea put forth by the Canadian journalist and author Malcolm Gladwell in his 2008 best seller, *Outliers*. In this book, Gladwell chronicles stories of those who excel at their craft, finding that one common denominator among such people is simply good, old-fashioned repetition: They each put in at least 10,000 hours of practice. Gladwell cites research carried out by psychologist K. Anders Ericsson and his colleagues, who examined the role of "deliberate practice" among violinists. They found that it took about ten years, or 10,000 hours of work, guided by a teacher or mentor, to gain mastery over their instruments. To do this sustainably, most of us need some level of passion for our field or craft.

Most people understand that intense interest in a field may alone not be enough to succeed or excel. We also need aptitude in the field(s) in which our passion(s) reside. However, a combination of passion and skills can still leave lower income professionals, like school teachers, struggling financially. As a result, we need to find a way to successfully monetize our skill set and passion, namely by figuring out how to add value to our colleagues, clients, community, and professional field in order to meet our financial goals.

The tendency to link passions to specific roles (like pro athletes, artists, and teachers) rather than traits helps reinforce the disconnect between our deep interests and what we end up doing to make a living. Furthermore, it doesn't help that we tend to evaluate jobs based on compensation. For example, we may love teaching but know that teachers don't earn much. As a result, those of us with more modest levels of interest and/or a higher lifestyle need are likely to discard passion in favor of earning. Instead of us pursuing this traditional and binary route, let's consider an alternate model that separates out optimizing our skill set and monetizing it to meet our lifestyle choice.

Skill Set Optimization

We already discussed a new way to apply passions to the workplace: Instead of focusing on the most classic role associated with something like art (artist) or sports (athlete), we instead encourage our children (and ourselves) to apply the transferable traits related to each.

Understanding and leveraging these traits can help us optimize a unique skill set that can apply to any number of career fields. In optimizing our skill set, I believe it helps to consider the following four key aspects about ourselves.

PASSION/INTEREST

My passion for psychology led me to introduce a financial product to the Singaporean market: target date funds, which reduces the need for people not interested in investment matters to engage actively and consistently with their retirement funds. In researching and proposing this solution, I came to a major realization about a passion-related topic: the foundational power of *interest* itself.

In short, target date funds serve to get around individual investors' lack of interest in investment-related matters. Granted, I understood that interest was only one part of the equation. The knowledge, interest, and time (KIT) study referenced in Chapter 7 compared levels of KIT related to financial matters among investors and found that disengaged investors lacked one, two, or all three.

So why focus primarily on interest, rather than on increasing investor knowledge or time? As I see it, a high level of interest serves to naturally boost the other two factors. If someone has interest in a topic, they will more readily make time for it, and thereby acquire knowledge about it. Sure, sometimes people learn out of necessity rather than interest, but since it's externally motivated rather than self-driven, necessity doesn't inspire us to constantly improve in the same way.

It was my own keen interest in psychology that prompted me to first dig deeper into the KIT study. This helped me reframe the issue, then direct our company efforts in the most impactful way. When we can infuse passion-related traits into our work lives, we get fresh insights and reach new levels of creativity that contribute to success.

APTITUDE

If I hadn't applied my own avid interest in learning about and solving people-related problems, I would never have innovated a financial product for the Singaporean market ahead of competitors. Still, as Mark Cuban and others have pointed out, interest or passion is not enough to guarantee success. We also need aptitude.

If we don't assess our aptitude appropriately, we could end up pursuing professional dead ends. For instance, if I lacked the ability to fully understand investment concepts, I wouldn't have been able to adapt target date funds from the US to better serve the local market and population in Singapore. Instead, I might have simply taken the product offered abroad and copied it wholesale (as one of our competitors did around the same time).

So how do we measure aptitude in ourselves or our children? It may seem overly simplistic, but we can learn a lot about what our aptitudes are and, just as importantly, how good we are at them based on what school subjects we excel in without much effort—from primary school through 12th grade. For example, when I first arrived in the US in fourth grade, my inherent quantitative skills resulted in my placement within an advanced math class of just three students, despite my not being able to speak English. As such, I can conclude that my aptitude was in numbers.

However, by my senior year of high school, I'd realized that calculus likely marked the upper bounds of my math skills. I'm sure that my relative lack of interest in advanced math played a part in setting this limit, but either way, it became abundantly clear that, unlike some of my classmates, I would not be going to MIT or Caltech on a math scholarship. My skills were above average at best. While my career path still leverages my math skills, this above-average aptitude nicely intersects with my interests, like solving people's problems and imparting knowledge to others.

UNIQUE FACTOR

This brings us to the third point of one's "unique factor." I define this as that which differentiates us from others with the same or higher levels of interest and aptitude. One of my unique factors is how I manage to apply my interest in psychology within the field of finance. Another relates to my teaching skills—namely, my ability to break down complex concepts and explain them to people at different levels of knowledge and sophistication. In my past sales-related roles, I would take the trouble of exploring issues my prospects and clients were concerned about, and then I'd use the expertise of my colleagues to impart knowledge (communicated at the appropriate level of sophistication) to help resolve these concerns. This consultative approach to sales, which leverages my unique factor, may not work for someone with less interest in investor behavior or teaching. However, based on my overall sales track record throughout my three decades in the industry, it has worked well for me.

Understanding my unique factor has helped me home in on the right clients and prospects for success. For example, I will likely not appeal to clients who like to be entertained, rather than informed. In other words, I'm the wrong person to go to for advice on which wine would pair best with filet mignon.

OPERATING STYLE

In every field, you'll find highly specialized experts, as well as versatile jacks-of-all-trades. Some dive very deep in just one or two areas throughout their careers. Others naturally dabble along the surface of a wide range of topics (the "jack-of-all-trades"). I refer to this as operating style, and it can help determine where and how a person thrives professionally.

Personally, I count myself among the well-rounded generalists, engaging with sufficient depth in a number of topics related to financial matters. This knowledge helps me serve client and prospect needs—while my more specialized colleagues in research or portfolio management delve deeper into balance sheets, company assessments, and market predictions.

Could I have become a portfolio manager? Perhaps. However, my broader operating style isn't naturally inclined to focus into the weeds of company financial statements, management performance indicators, and industry trends to select those companies that will outperform its peers. Neither would I enjoy simply selling an off-the-shelf financial product to unsophisticated investors. I prefer engaging prospects and clients a bit deeper. As such, I'd put my operating style at about 60 percent general, 40 percent specialized.

Although there's no guarantee of success, this approach of optimizing these four factors allowed me to excel for 30-plus years in an industry that largely compensates based on product sales. By applying my interests, aptitude, unique factor, and operating style within one field, I optimized my skill set far beyond what I might have achieved hopping from one field or role to the other, in search of my "true" passion.

Monetization

Related to skill set optimization is the matter of how to best monetize these factors—especially for those of us still learning to crystalize those Entrepreneur and Investor Mindsets.

In other words, how do we best turn our optimal skills into new or supplementary income streams? When it comes to monetization, most professionals with the traditional Employee Mindset take the approach of taking a salaried job at a company or organization. However, the most traditional, literal application of one's passion is not always the most viable, marketable, or profitable way to go. For example, someone with a $$$ lifestyle level would not be satisfied with a school teacher's salary, despite having a passion for imparting knowledge.

As such a young person who loves teaching but understands the limited earning potential of the traditional classroom may abandon this passion altogether. However, I find that when people understand how to apply their interests, aptitudes, unique factors, and operating styles to their chosen field, it becomes easier for them to develop more of a "true" Entrepreneur Mindset. Such a mindset is key to driving new ideas that target unmet market needs. Doing so can accelerate both their professional growth and their earning potential.

Let's consider a hypothetical school teacher who's somewhat specialized with a passion for helping children with learning disabilities progress and realize their potential. She also has an extremely high aptitude for science, and her unique factor has to do with her ability to customize her teaching approach to work with each child's learning style. For children with short attention spans, she breaks material into chunks and tells colorful stories. Meanwhile, she helps other students learn through hands-on activities, or maybe visual models. Over time, this top-tier school teacher develops a unique set of techniques to teach science to a wide range of students, especially those who struggle with more traditional learning methods.

Having optimized her skill set, this teacher can now consider a number of options in regards to monetizing it. If she's happy with a $ lifestyle level, she may simply continue her work as a public school teacher. However, she could increase her lifestyle to the $$ level by seeking employment in a private school, and/or supplementing her teaching job with a side gig like private tutoring. Maybe that leads to her creating educational social media content that she can monetize further. To earn above the $$ lifestyle level, she might also invest in education-related companies. She could also operate an educational franchise or even set up her own tuition center, employing other teachers to utilize the methodology she developed. Taken to the next level, she could then franchise her own tuition center, or sell the business itself.

PASSION GAP PEOPLE

Skill Set Optimization	Monetization
♡ Passion/Interest	$ $ $ $ $ Business Owner and Investor
💡 Aptitude	$ $ $ $ Investor or Business Owner
👀 Unique Factor	$ $ $ Employee, Side Gig, and Investor
⚙ Operating Style	$ $ Employee and Side Gig
	$ Employee

Although going beyond a traditional teaching job (with or without a side gig) requires more time and start-up capital—and represents dealing with uncertainties—doing so can create the potential to generate much greater income. While finding a side gig or setting up a social media following may be accessible to many, becoming an investor and/or business owner require both overcoming obstacles to taking the first step and a different mindset, which I believe everyone can, to some extent, cultivate for themselves (see Chapter 6).

Losing a stable income can be emotionally destabilizing. It brought back memories of the panic I felt after experiencing two consecutive layoffs during the early part of my career in the US. This time, however, I had my primary North Star in place to keep me on path. Rather than prematurely leaving my job, as I might have earlier in my career, I stuck it out, embracing the physician's words that a job is a means to that end. This not only helped me support my family's lifestyle, but it also taught me to adapt and allowed me to begin separating my identity from my career.

Meanwhile, I'd adopted a Financial Independence Mindset through my property and investment portfolios. I've also set up my own consulting firm to help investment management companies looking to enter the Asia Pacific markets, and I'm sitting on corporate boards. Setting up these streams of income enabled me to not have to rely on a traditional job to meet my and my children's lifestyle requirements.

So while losing stable income brought on angst, I felt prepared and, in many ways, relieved—even a bit excited for how I could next apply my interests and live my values. This was only made possible because I was able to close my Passion Gap.

TAKEAWAYS

If you're wondering whether to pursue passion or money, you're asking the wrong question. It isn't about *whether* you can have one or the other, but rather about *how* and *when* you can close your personal Passion Gap to claim both.

Of course, if you've inherited a fortune (or at least a sizable trust fund), or you're born into some rare, exceptional gift allowing you to rise to the top of your field that also pays exceptionally well—then, by all means, unabashedly pursue that passion right away. Likewise if you're content to live out of a camper as a $ lifestyle down-to-earther, or if you would wither and die without your art, go ahead and chase what lights you up.

However, I believe the majority of us need a little more self-analysis and a solid strategy to close our Passion Gap over time. To begin, we need to get honest about our preferred lifestyle levels; assess our interests, aptitudes, operating styles, and unique factors; and put in the work to both optimize and monetize our skill sets. Depending on your specific answers to these questions, it could take a few years to close your Passion Gap—or it could take several decades.

If I had the opportunity, I'd ask Mark Cuban whether it's possible that he had dismissed his passion because he had mistakenly tied "passion" to the job of an NBA player. I wonder if he would agree that certain traits he developed through early sports training—discipline, competitiveness, focus, teamwork, leadership—are the very characteristics that have made him a successful entrepreneur. Successful enough, in fact, for him to truly become a "player" within the field of professional basketball, albeit on the business end.

The trick (or one of them) is true self-awareness. Do you truly have what it takes to pursue passion now? Do you have the natural aptitude, motivation level, and risk tolerance to meaningfully compete with the world's leading athletes or artists? Are you willing to make the necessary sacrifices? If not, try examining what your passions reveal about your transferable interests. Then optimize them with your aptitudes, unique factors, and operating styles.

Another way to speed up the process of closing your Passion Gap is to reconsider the lifestyle level you "need" to feel comfortable and content. It turns out that I, for example, never needed a collection of expensive designer watches. I realize now that, to afford the lifestyle I thought I needed, I ended up traveling extensively (and unhappily) for years within a regional sales role. While this helped me to optimize (and certainly monetize) my skills, it also pulled me away from my true North Star of Serving Family.

As we explored in Chapter 6, another way to close the gap quicker is to diversify both your income streams through adopting additional earning mindsets. Rather than assuming that we can only work and earn as employees, I believe that we all can and should develop both the Investor and Entrepreneur Mindsets as well—albeit to different degrees and proportions, depending on our level of drive and interests.

So, how do we reconcile all this stuff about jobs, money, and passion with the opening subject of this book: finding and sustaining happiness over the long term?

I believe that the final step toward achieving a life of lasting happiness will help us integrate everything we've covered in these first eight chapters in order to build a life rich in both purpose and meaning—two different but related topics that we'll address in the next and final chapter.

LEARNING POINTS

- *Passion Now* people are those lucky few who can immediately pursue professional passions without concern for money, whether due to inherited wealth, very modest lifestyle needs, or rare, prodigious talent.

- For the rest of us *Passion Gap* people, it takes time, self-awareness, and effort to integrate our professional passions while maintaining our preferred lifestyle levels.

- By understanding, optimizing, and monetizing the skill sets related to your primary interests and related traits, you can more quickly and effectively bridge your Passion Gap.

- It's not about choosing between passion and money, but about how and when you can have both.

SELF-REFLECTION

- Are you a Passion Now or Passion Gap person?

- How would you measure or define your aptitude, "unique factor," and operating style—and how can you optimize and monetize these passion-related skill sets to close your Passion Gap?

9

FINDING MEANING, PURPOSE, AND LASTING HAPPINESS

Life has no meaning. Each of us has meaning and we bring it to life.
It is a waste to be asking the question when you are the answer.

—Joseph Campbell

"Dad didn't really leave much of a mark on the world."

This statement came from my friend and former colleague KW, after his father had passed away. He was processing a conversation with his two brothers about their father's legacy—or, as they saw it, his apparent lack thereof.

The death of KW's father didn't attract media attention. There were no processions or lengthy eulogies. Life simply went on: The sun rose and set as the world went on turning, same as before. There was, however, one notable exception: KW's elderly mother, who felt utterly lost without her late husband.

"Mom doesn't drive and doesn't know how to do a lot of things around the house, mainly because Dad was happy to do everything for her," he said. To KW and his brothers, it seemed that this man, who'd thrown all his efforts into caring for their family, had otherwise lived a small and unremarkable life. He was unquestionably a loving husband and father, but had his life been one of purpose or meaning?

This brought to mind my own father, who'd passed away when I was 24 and living a thousand miles away. Those final months of his life were not all I'd missed. In fact, I have very few memories of my dad.

At the age of 43, my dad moved to a foreign land with a wife, four children, and a seemingly insurmountable cultural-linguistic rift. Through our church sponsors, my dad landed a job at Nabisco, first as a night janitor and later as a second-shift quality assurance worker.

My own father, it seemed, had left even less of a legacy—at least, in terms of some illustrious "mark on the world"—than KW's. Mainly, I remember Dad either lying in bed or emerging in pajamas and disheveled hair as he tried to replenish an endless sleep deficit.

Like KW's dad—who hustled to keep up with the rapid economic growth of the newly independent Singapore—my own father faced considerable challenges. In short, neither my father nor KW's had the luxury of pursuing much in terms of "purpose in life"—aside from providing opportunities for their children while trying not to go under.

Does that mean my father's life had little meaning? What about my own? This question occurs to most people at some point. Assuming we live long and thoughtfully enough, we'll eventually wonder how our families, friends, and associates will remember us when we're gone. Will they measure our impact in terms of whether or not crowds of mourners observe our deaths? If so, does that mean the majority of us live lives void of meaning or purpose?

In this final chapter, we'll look at these two concepts, how they fit together with the other concepts explored in this book—and, most importantly, how we can practically apply it all to our quest for lasting happiness.

DEFINING LIFE'S PURPOSE AND MEANING

You could argue that some questions we've explored—like how to follow your passion without starving, or whether to look for some higher meaning through a job—are matters that only more modern and privileged humans have the luxury to contemplate. I don't think it's a coincidence that these topics are so hotly debated in the United States, a nation that (despite large and growing economic disparities) continues to promote the "American dream" of flashy individual success, endless possibilities, and the constitutionally protected "pursuit of happiness."

However, when it comes to the meaning and purpose of an individual's *life* itself, we arrive at a much more universal line of questioning, crossing the globe and stretching back millenniums. Whether or not the ancient Greek philosopher Aristotle used these same terms, what we're trying to uncover is how to define and realize our life's meaning and purpose in a way that gets us closer to his notion of *eudaimonia*, or lasting happiness that aligns with one's highest virtues.

Like any early 21st-century seeker, I turned to Google. I began by typing, "What is the meaning of life?" and "What is your life's purpose?" This brought up 11.3 billion and 6.0 billion results, respectively. Theologians, philosophers, academics, psychologists, and self-help gurus—not to mention apparently billions of everyday people—have puzzled over these questions. Still, there seems to be no consensus on what these words mean, or even about whether purpose and meaning are, in fact, synonyms or two distinct ideas.

I get it—unpacking and defining terms like these can seem like a Herculean task. As with most vague, broad, and/or lofty concepts (e.g., happiness, prosperity, passion), there seem to be no universally agreed upon definitions for "meaning" or "purpose"—at least, not when applied to life itself.

After sampling what philosophers, experts, and authors think, I've come to my own conclusions, which I hope may serve (or, at the very least, entertain) my children, as well as anyone else still along for the ride.

In short, life's meaning and purpose are, I believe, two different—if deeply interconnected—aspects of each individual human experience. They further vary from person to person, and they're related to ideas explored in previous chapters—namely, our North Stars, lifestyle levels, and Passion Gap profiles.

Now, let's take a look at some of the studies, theories, and advice I found related to life's meaning and purpose before offering my perspective.

Life's Meaning

It seems the question of the "meaning of life" got a lot of attention from 19th- and 20th-century philosophers. Modernism and logical positivism both offered rational, scientific counters to mystical, supernatural sensibilities. The postmodernists argued instead that life offered few (if any) absolute, objective truths. Finally, existentialists proclaimed that life was void of inherent meaning; it was up to individuals to create life's meaning for themselves.

Existentialism's more subjective approach seems to have heavily influenced modern thinking, including the Holocaust survivor Viktor Frankl. In his 1946 classic, *Man's Search for Meaning*, Frankl wrote that "the meaning of life differs from man to man, from day to day, and from hour to hour. What matters, therefore, is not the meaning of life in general but rather the specific meaning of a person's life at a given moment." Frankl's experience of living through a Nazi concentration camp taught him that perspective is a choice, and that every individual creates his or her own meaning—even within the most hopeless and miserable conditions.

Much more recently—in 2021—Joshua Hicks and Laura King, psychology professors at Texas A&M University and the University of Missouri, respectively, published a paper titled "The Science of Meaning in Life." Like the existentialists, these professors viewed meaning in life as a "subjective experience"—one composed of three facets: comprehension/coherence, purpose, and existential mattering/significance. In other words, the belief that your life makes sense, that it has a purpose, and that it matters.

Hicks and King concluded that a person's sense of "comprehension/coherence" tends to be rooted in predictable or logical patterns, outcomes, and routines. However, when life gets confusing, one's "purpose" can provide the clarity and resilience needed to persevere. Finally, they found that people's sense of "significance"—that they *matter*—appears most heavily influenced by social factors. Their paper closes with the following insight: "Trying to understand why our life is meaningful may serve a function when life becomes incomprehensible, but ultimately it may never yield a satisfying answer. Meaning is not just found in one place. It is all around us—in our relationships, work, and spiritual and religious beliefs, as well as through the appreciating of life itself."

Life's Purpose

Recently, the Japanese term "ikigai" has garnered international attention, following the 2017 publication of *Ikigai: The Japanese Secret to a Long and Happy Life*. The book's co-authors, Hector Garcia and Francesc Miralles, define "ikigai" as one's reason for being/living. Their approach seems to focus largely on how to achieve this state through one's vocation, as they locate ikigai at the "intersection of what you love, what the world needs, what you're good at, and what you can be paid for."

For those interested in a more spiritual—specifically, Christian—approach, Rick Warren's best seller *The Purpose Driven Life* describes what he sees as God's five purposes for human life: Christian worship, fellowship, discipleship, ministry, and mission. In contrast to the subjectivity we saw in existential interpretations of "life's meaning," Warren advises his readers against focusing on themselves. Instead, he insists that life's *purpose* can only be found through God.

On the other hand—in sharp contrast to this theological view—we have Mark Manson. This American author of the 2016 book *The Subtle Art of Not Giving a F*ck* offered the following (rather blunt) perspective: "Part of the problem is the concept of 'life purpose' itself. The idea that we were each born for some higher purpose and it's now our cosmic mission to find it. This is the same kind of sh***y logic used to justify things like spirit crystals or that your lucky number is 34 (but only on Tuesdays or during full moons)." Putting aside his skepticism toward idealism and spirituality, Manson's definition of life's purpose seems to boil down to each person doing what they deem most important with the time they have—which brings us back to a more subjective, individually defined approach.

While I could go on and on about different popular interpretations of life's purpose, let's close out this section with nationally recognized author and coach Richard Leider, author of the best seller *The Power of Purpose*. He argues that every individual's true purpose is to identify their unique gifts, passions, and values—and then utilize those to give back to the world through some kind of service. Leider's definition resonated with me, although I see the equation slightly differently.

So, is purpose a part of meaning, or is meaning a part of purpose? Are they one and the same, or two separate and/or interconnected concepts? (If you're like me, your head may be spinning right now.)

When initially researching this chapter, I discussed my confusion with a young lawyer acquaintance. At the time, I admittedly assumed the two concepts were one and the same. That changed after I explained my thinking to her.

"What about giving back to society?" she asked. "There's got to be more when it comes to our meaning or purpose in life than just ourselves and our families."

At that moment, I realized I was viewing these concepts through the lens of my own North Star values, specifically my Polaris A of Serving Family. Her perspective reminded me of an article I'd read on Ariana Huffington's digital platform *Thrive Global*, dedicated to behavioral change and technology. The article began with the following line: "The combination of a successful career, a loving family, and a strong social network can seem like the recipe for a perfect life. However, even those who can check each of these boxes might feel that something is missing—and that 'something' is their life's purpose."[1] Could this be hinting about our Polaris Ab?

When I thought through my own struggles of finding meaning and purpose, I realized that those with a primary North Star of Serving God or Serving Society largely experience little doubt about what they were placed on earth to do. In fact, for these individuals, purpose and meaning are closely intertwined, if not, one and the same. Family is simply part and parcel of a larger plan for them.

Sure, the conviction levels of such individuals may differ. For example, Eleanor is unlikely to make the same sacrifices to her Polaris Ab (her family) as compared to Pastor K. Likewise, Pastor K may not have taken Bonhoeffer's life sacrificing actions. Nonetheless, these individuals share the same world view: Their calling to serve is inevitable and not to be questioned or rationalized.

I am, therefore, addressing the remainder of this chapter to those (who I believe make up the majority among us) whose primary North Star is Serving Family. I'll also assume that most of us, especially those of younger generations, will have both a primary (Polaris A) and a secondary (Polaris Ab) North Star. Let's now explore these two concepts as I view them.

MEANING AS INNER SIGNIFICANCE

I'd originally defined "meaning" and "purpose" as synonyms describing something more internally focused. Namely, a sense of life's meaning influenced by aspirations (lifestyle and vocation), traits, and interests (passion), but—above all—shaped by North Star values, which, for me, happen to focus on Serving Family. This self-examination led me to define what makes life meaningful—for me, personally. But what if there was a second element we could call "purpose," that's based on the *external impact* we leave on the world, beyond home and family? What about that "something missing" to which both my lawyer acquaintance and *Thrive Global* alluded?

Suddenly I felt much clearer about my definition of "meaning." I now see it as the highly personalized *inner significance* of one's life, focused on their primary North Star (Polaris A) and balanced out by their aspirations, strengths/traits, and interests. I also better understand now how to distinguish that from purpose as our *external impact* on the world (which I'll get to in a moment).

Coincidentally, "meaning" starts with "me"—which, to me, emphasizes the subjectivity of life's meaning for every distinct individual. In other words, "meaning" is all about *me*. It's about what makes my life feel significant and worthwhile, which for me is ultimately rooted in the guiding value of my primary North Star of Serving Family. This source of meaning—family—may technically be something outside of myself, but it's still derived from something very personal and intimately connected to me, especially compared to the externally focused value of Serving Society (my Polaris Ab).

In short, we achieve meaning in life when we're able to align the following four key aspects of what matters to each of us—those topics covered from Chapters 2 to 8.

The "Why"

Since my mid-40s, when I realized that Serving Family is my primary North Star, I've attempted to align my life decisions to this guiding light. I haven't always done a perfect job, and life events have a way of distracting or obscuring one's primary North Star at times. Still, having that goal of doing what's best for my two children always drives me to get up each morning and never give up.

Again, Serving Family represents a more internally focused value compared to that of Serving Society. This means that, when it comes to what will bring me the most lasting happiness, I'm more oriented toward meaning than purpose. It also suggests that, to maximize my lasting happiness, my purpose (my external impact on society) actually *should* take a back seat to my guiding core value of supporting the best possible life and future for my family.

Those who prioritize Serving Society or Serving God as their primary North Stars may find the action and significance of their lives more directed by their calling. For example, when my friend Eleanor sacrificed both her free time and higher potential pay, her actions demonstrated how Serving God outweighed the more internally focused value of Serving Family. As a result, she is content with giving up a lot when it comes to her family's lifestyle, our next topic.

Lifestyle Implications

As noted in earlier chapters, reflecting on what makes life feel meaningful (or purposeful) can help anchor us, but it won't equate to much if we're not able to support ourselves or our families financially. Specifically, once we realize the value of service toward something greater than the self (family, society, or God), we can more thoughtfully allocate our resources to align with our priorities.

This is certainly true in my case. Despite the material temptations I see working in the finance industry (not to mention living in one of the most expensive cities in the world), understanding my $$$ lifestyle requirements has recalibrated my relationship with spending. This approach keeps me from falling into the traps of lifestyle creep that affect many around me, including some who earn less than I do.

I also make conscious financial trade-offs within my lifestyle requirements, for example, spending less on vacations, clothing, and entertainment in order to prioritize the cost of a home in a nicer area for my kids' schooling and future financial security. In short, by assessing my lifestyle needs and adjusting my habits and expectations, I've managed to protect and provide for the aspect of my life that brings me the greatest sense of meaning: my children. While doing this, I've further learned to balance our next two topics: making a living and pursuing my passion.

Making a Living

I learned early in my career that income from traditional jobs can be fleeting, especially in light of layoffs. In fact, they happen with each economic cycle—or whenever they might benefit shareholders and senior management financially incentivized by a healthier share price. Part of why it's so important to get grounded and realistic about lifestyle has to do with the unreliability of our changing global job market and its impact on income sustainability. In Chapter 4, we discussed how most companies don't typically have a significant "purpose" beyond profits (despite their marketing and recruitment rhetoric). As long as shareholders maintain their short-term interests in reported company earnings, decisions—including those that seriously impact their staffing—will be made accordingly.

In short, to fully live one's meaning (Serving Family) and/or purpose (Serving Society/God) in life, while maintaining our lifestyle, we need to protect ourselves from such job market and income fluctuations.

Granted, diversifying income may not directly add inherent *meaning* or *purpose* to your life. However, it can help us realize the meaning/purpose of our lives by both insulating ourselves against financial variables and helping us bridge our Passion Gap.

Bridging the Passion Gap

Again, by closing/bridging the Passion Gap, I don't (necessarily) mean ranking among the top 450 basketball players in the world. Instead, I'm talking about understanding your own personal traits (skills, proficiencies, and attributes) and strong interests, then balancing those against your preferred lifestyle level and figuring out how those traits and interests might transfer into an optimum career. Then it's a matter of learning how to monetize this skill set in order to generate the level of income needed to sustainably meet your desired lifestyle.

For example, my passions include understanding and solving complex people issues and imparting knowledge to others. I've managed to combine these unique factors with my aptitude for numbers and my operating style to help me optimize and monetize my skill set within my chosen career field of finance.

Once I generate enough passive income from my investments to support my $$$ lifestyle beyond simply working for someone else, I can turn my full attention to conducting workshops, even writing more books, and, of course, spending more time with my two children. I can continue to work in the investment management industry, either through traditional employment or by setting up my own shop to advise investment management firms looking to enter the region. The key is that my next steps can be based on a choice rather than a need.

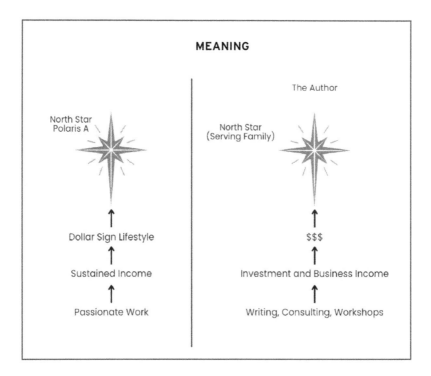

To me, closing the Passion Gap allows me to realize my meaning in life: simply waking up every morning loving what I do and having a sustainable level of income to support the preferred lifestyle for me and my two children.

PURPOSE AS EXTERNAL IMPACT

The reason why I find the author Richard Leider's definition of "gifts + passions + values = purpose" to be a useful guide is that he alludes to many of the same attributes as I do. In some ways, it reflects my own logic of how to achieve external impact (purpose)—at least for those of us whose primary North Star is grounded by Serving Family.

However, my equation differs slightly: "optimized skill set + passions → Polaris Ab = purpose."

Since Serving Society ranks as my secondary North Star—my Polaris Ab—then my *purpose* is simply to donate my optimized skill set in areas that I'm passionate about to serving others.

For example, let's consider my friend SY. SY has always had a passion for both photography and teaching. Since retiring from a global investment organization, he teaches financial risk management (his optimized skill set) as an adjunct professor (his passion) at a local university. He also took photography classes and now offers photography services (his passion) to clients. Since his Polaris Ab is Serving Society, he set up his photography business as a nonprofit. SY's clients can choose among several nonprofit organizations to which they donate his fees.

For those (less common) individuals naturally most inclined toward Serving God or Serving Society as their primary North Star, serving others will play a much larger role in their lives than Serving Family. To Pastor K, for example, Serving God meant sacrificing a great deal of his and his family's financial opportunities and lifestyle. Individuals like Pastor K tend to end up (as KW put it that day in his office) leaving more of a "mark on the world" than most. We can view how much we lean into our purpose as our external "impact score."

For example, people like Mandela, Bonhoeffer, and even Pastor K would have a much higher external impact score than a guy like me, who's mainly just trying to be a good dad and give back to society where and when I can. I'd say that someone willing to spend 27 years in jail in pursuit of social justice should earn a full ten out of ten when it comes to impact on society.

The level of conviction we have for our sources of lasting happiness can help us determine what external impact score we can safely aspire to. For example, if I had to allocate my conviction level between my two North Star values, I'd put Serving Family at 70 percent and Serving Society at 30 percent. If we applied the same ratio to impact scores, that would put my external impact score at a humble three.

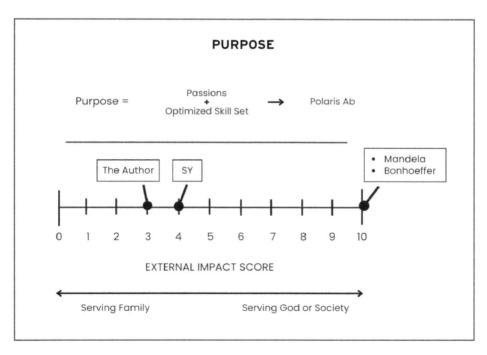

My friend SY, whom you may recall from Chapter 3, has a stronger conviction to Serving Society as compared to me. He would score more like 60 percent Serving Family and 40 percent Serving Society. His impact score would be around a four.

Similar to the exercise on determining our lifestyle dollar sign, we're not trying to split hairs here. An approximation of our external impact score can help us to better understand what makes us tick and how we differ (not better or worse) from those around us. In this instance, our external impact score offers insight into the significance of our secondary North Star—our Polaris Ab—relative to our primary one.

I do, however, strongly suggest that you avoid selecting five as your external impact score. The reason for doing so is that it challenges you to further examine your priorities, rather than just sitting on the fence.

Although my score or SY's may not sound impressive when compared to those of Bonhoeffer or Mandela, I believe it's perfectly acceptable for most of us to remain content with prioritizing our life's meaning. The key lesson is to recognize that we don't have to (and shouldn't) live up to someone else's external impact score but our own.

ACHIEVING LASTING HAPPINESS THROUGH BALANCE

After getting clear on what brings meaning and purpose to our lives, including our external impact score, we still need to strike the right balance between the two if we want to achieve lasting happiness. To illustrate what it means to balance meaning and purpose, let's review my own situation. My primary North Star (Polaris A) is Serving Family, and my secondary priority (Polaris Ab) is Serving Society. For me to find and live my meaning in life, I first need to recognize and prioritize those values. To better support this North Star constellation, I can optimize my skill set and define my passion in order to better serve both (primarily) family and (secondarily) society.

I believe that for most of us, Serving Family represents our primary North Star—even though some (like me) don't realize it right away. This means that it's perfectly acceptable for us to have a purpose-driven impact score of below five, as long as we're focused on building meaning aligned with our guiding values. The key is to understand these values and how much time, money, and effort we're willing to redirect *away* from our life's meaning in order to pursue our purpose (and vice versa).

As exceptions like Mandela and Bonhoeffer demonstrate, there are no right or wrong answers. Pastor K, for example, was willing to spend two years away from his family and forgo material comforts in order to further his seminary studies—something I could never conceive of doing as a father.

We must also recognize that while our circumstances will change as we navigate different stages of life, our external impact score will largely remain the same. For example, after E and S were born, I seriously reconsidered how and where I spent my extra time. This meant walking away from community volunteer efforts I'd previously engaged in. I felt absolutely no guilt for doing so at the time. As my children grow older—and now that I've managed to bridge my Passion Gap—I'm able to increase the amount of time and resources I can comfortably dedicate to Serving Society (my Polaris Ab) again. However, I have no doubt that if S or E should need me for whatever reason, I would again drop my social services activities to be there for them.

For those of us without a high external impact score, we must keep our life's meaning intact. In so doing, I believe that we do fulfill our designated purpose within society, as KW's father has shown. After all, society functions best when people can thrive within harmonious, loving homes and families. In this way, I think of one's life meaning as the bedrock that allows us to (indirectly) contribute to society and thereby fulfill some of our purpose as well.

If we pursue our purpose at the expense of our meaning (typically, our families and home lives), we'll end up regretting the sacrifices made to our primary North Star, whether through strained relationships, divorce, or financial problems. The key is to get clear on where we stand between our meaning (Polaris A) and purpose (Polaris Ab). For example, if I were to attempt an external impact score higher than three, I would feel off-kilter and likely regret the sacrifices I'd be making when it comes to my children.

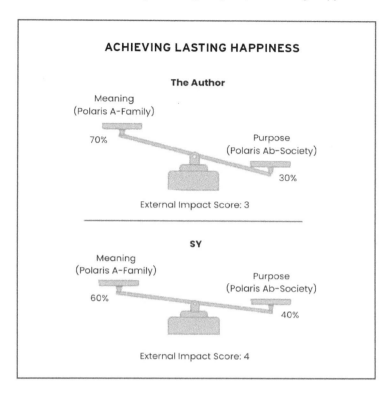

BACK TO ARISTOTLE AND EUDAIMONIA

As we close out this final chapter, I offer a final tribute to Aristotle, whose musings on the notion of *eudaimonia* greatly influenced my understanding of a lasting happiness rooted in meaning (inner significance) and purpose (external impact).

You may recall that Aristotle broke down his notion of eudaimonia into the following levels of happiness: *Laetus*, derived from material objects; *Felix*, from ego gratification; *Beautitudo*, from doing good for others; and finally *Sublime Beautitudo*, a transcendent state attained by achieving a balance of the three levels, and "finding your own calling."

While material objects and "ego gratification" seem to describe more fleeting, *hedonic* sources of happiness, Aristotle acknowledged that material comforts (laetus) and the satisfaction of personal achievement and recognition (felix) have their rightful place.

I agree. That's also why so much of this book focuses on understanding what levels of financial and professional success you need to factor into your own unique equation for achieving lasting happiness.

I'd say following your passion (felix) while earning enough to balance your preferred lifestyle level (laetus)—both relate to that sense of inner significance, or *meaning*, in life. However, recall that the more important aspect of meaning, as I define it, involves balancing these aspects with your North Star values, which tend to involve *service to others*—whether to society or God.

This takes us to beautitudo, derived from doing good for others. To me, this informs our notion of purpose as external impact—that deeper well-being that comes from affecting change in the world by doing good for others.

So, what do we make of this final level, sublime beautitudo, that most transcendent, sustained happiness? Ultimately, this describes a balance among all of the above: securing your preferred lifestyle through professional and material achievement, pursuing your deeper passions, and—most importantly—rooting your life in the North Star values of service to others.

That all-important balance is what helps us self-actualize and "find our own calling" through sublime beautitudo. Most of us cannot arrive to this level of transcendent, lasting happiness through job titles and designer watches alone, nor through solely martyring ourselves for others with little personal gain.

To build a life of meaning as inner significance while leaving a positive impact on the world through purpose, we need to find this balance, which reflects who we are as individuals. And we find that through deep introspection.

If we do that, we can live our lives according to Aristotle's notion of eudaimonia, the *state of being* achieved through living a balanced and virtuous life—and the term that ultimately inspired this book's journey.

It wasn't easy for KW and myself to process the fact that our fathers didn't leave significant marks on the world—especially when reminded of the Bonhoeffers and Mandelas of the world. However, even beyond understanding who we are, we must also acknowledge the cards that we've been dealt. Compared to our fathers, KW and I actually have the luxury of pursuing some purpose beyond providing for our families, not to mention our passions when doing so.

That day in KW's office, I shared stories about my own late father and asked whether his father faced similar limitations. After I finished, I saw tears well up in my friend's eyes. Adopting a different perspective, KW could more clearly see the limits of measuring the meaning and purpose of a life solely in terms of external societal impact. In fact, it suddenly became clear just how powerful of a legacy each of these men left behind—legacies that we can honor and pass on by caring for our own families in turn. Legacies that will allow us, and the generations that follow, to pay it forward to society where they couldn't.

TAKEAWAYS

Aside from recognizing our individual meaning and purpose in life, we must each achieve the right balance between these two. My goal is that what I've proposed in this chapter will help E, S, and whoever else may be reading to achieve that "transcendent" state of long-term happiness Aristotle spoke of millenniums ago.

While it can be fun to philosophize, at the end of the day, I prefer definitions that are practical, simple, and applied. For the majority of us, I define life's meaning as internally focused on Serving Family and providing the life we want for our families, while still feeding our passion. Purpose is more externally focused. It's about Serving God or Serving Society in a way that also utilizes our skills and passions to leave a positive direct impact on the world. However, there will always be a built-in tension in terms of a trade-off between the two—be it money, energy, or time invested into each.

The most important lesson to take away is that there's no one-size-fits-all answer when it comes to the matter of legacy. As with KW's father, or my own, we don't always have the resources, skills, or drive to leave a high direct impact score on the external world. There's no need to feel shame or guilt if you're not as devoted as Bonhoeffer was to Serving God, or as Mandela was to Serving Society. However, when we do have the capacity to give back, we should all strive to do so to the best of our abilities, while understanding and respecting the constraints of our financial and family lives. We all leave a different mark on the world.

LEARNING POINTS

- I define *meaning* as the inner significance you cultivate when doing what you love (passion) and achieving your preferred lifestyle level (income), while serving your primary North Star value.

- *Purpose* is more externally focused on serving and giving back to others. Your purpose, measured by your individual external *impact score*, aligns directly with your secondary North Star.

- Achieving lasting happiness means living a life that balances meaning with purpose, in line with your external impact scores.

- By aligning professional and personal goals with your North Stars, you can leave a unique mark on the world, regardless of your external impact score.

SELF-REFLECTION

- How would you define your inner meaning, based on your unique balance of passions, desired income, and values?

- What is your external impact score—based not on ego or comparison to others, but on your guiding North Star values?

CONCLUSION

I began this book—indeed, this whole exploration into meaning, purpose, passion, and prosperity—with the simple question of what parents want for their kids. My personal answer, and the one I most commonly hear from other parents, seems simple.

In a word, *happiness*.

As it turns out, that's a lot to unpack. We want our children to lead happy lives—to see them not just healthy and gainfully employed, but also flourishing. We want their lives rich in meaning and purpose and illuminated by their passions. And of course, we don't want them to have to sacrifice health or material security to achieve any of that.

At the very least, we want them to avoid our mistakes and not inherit our emotional baggage. As I sat in that family therapist's office months before becoming a father, I reevaluated my views and values around everything from meaning to money, and how it all connects to happiness.

Preparing to welcome my first child reminded me of my earliest and, indeed, quite happy memories of Cambodia. We were comfortable, stable, and surrounded by family—until our family's hasty retreat from the only home I'd ever known. We flew empty-handed to refugee camps before settling in the "land of opportunity."

The American idea of pursuing happiness pervaded my early education in Portland. But while teachers told us to follow our dreams and reach for the stars, I struggled to reconcile that message with the shame of peer rejection and material lack.

I had no idea what "my passion" might be.

All I knew was that, when I grew up, I did *not* want to be poor. It's perhaps no wonder that I gravitated toward an urban youth culture of acting out and showing off. In short, I rebelled, falling into a self-destructive cycle of parties, alcohol, and other short-lived hedonism.

While I eventually shaped up, earned several good degrees, and entered a lucrative industry, I still had no idea how to "find my passion," let alone meaning or purpose. Instead, I pursued "happiness" through earning money—to blow on luxury items I didn't need to impress people who didn't really care.

FINDING MY "WHY"

By early adulthood, I was back in Asia, a young finance professional—rootless, cynical about family, reckless with spending, and overall deeply unhappy. At this point, *following passion*—that theme from my American childhood—resurfaced in my mind. I knew my life lacked . . . something. *Maybe*, I thought, *I should go back and earn the psychology degree . . . or at least find a firm driven by values more aligned with my own.*

It didn't yet occur to me to cultivate meaning and purpose within my personal life. In part because I barely had one. Work consumed nearly every waking hour. I also had never considered that my passions—including my interest in human psychology and knack for instructing others—might offer transferable traits I could apply to my career in finance, and/or develop into entrepreneurial side pursuits.

In short, I deeply wanted to reconcile notions of "passion" with my need to earn a living, but I had no idea how.

By the time I reached out to that fatherly physician for advice on the matter, I lacked any meaningful concept of home, except as a place to sleep between work hours. I certainly hadn't given much thought to getting married or having kids.

While I had a vague sense of wanting to live a better life, I had no internal compass for how to do that. No concept of a North Star. No idea that the answer to my elusive search for happiness might actually lie in something as fundamental (and, to me, elusive) as family and home.

The physician's response was short and to the point. As he saw it, I was looking for happiness in all the wrong places. *Real* happiness, he claimed—the kind that actually *lasts*—is rooted in service. Some find it through Serving God, perhaps as a clergy member. Others find it through Serving Society as a humanitarian activist. The rest find it within that most basic social unit: Serving Family.

Following that doctor's advice about happiness as service—and an unlikely Angelina Jolie–related epiphany—I finally became a father myself. E's and S's arrivals confirmed my primary North Star of Serving Family and inspired in me a deep desire to better understand how to live a good life and help my children and others do the same.

Those prenatal counseling sessions, meant to prevent my passing emotional baggage to my children, were just the start. Fatherhood inspired me to launch a journey of discovery, seeking expert and popular advice from books, articles, and studies on everything from long-term happiness to income sustainability to passion, meaning, and purpose—all of which culminated in this book you're holding now.

ACHIEVING LASTING HAPPINESS

As it turns out, achieving lasting happiness is not as mysterious or complex as I once thought. It simply comes down to learning who you are by asking the right questions.

First, we need to know our guiding motivation: the *why*. This comes down to knowing your primary North Star, be it Serving Family, Serving God, or Serving Society (along with, for most of us, a secondary core value, or Polaris Ab). Since the most powerful *why* comes down to service, answering that question also illuminates the most important *who* and/or *what* in our lives.

With our North Stars in hand, we turn to figuring out how much money is enough to bring contentment when providing for ourselves and those we serve. With the *why* (i.e., *who/what*), and *how much* in place, our next task is to focus on generating the income to sustain the lifestyle level we desire. In our rapidly changing global workplace—increasingly marked by job insecurity, AI, contract work, and international outsourcing—*how* do we achieve income sustainability?

The answer here is threefold. First, stay away from the Joneses! Avoiding the trappings of lifestyle creep helps us maintain our lifestyle levels while we adapt to our constantly changing professional landscape.

Secondly, we need to adopt a Financial Independence Mindset in order to both survive and thrive. This means examining how we've been conditioned into an Employee Mindset by school and society, and learning to adopt elements of both the Investor and Entrepreneur Mindsets, including the "true" entrepreneurial practice of identifying problems and innovating solutions, whether in a business or salaried position.

Finally, we need to overcome the all too common reluctance to take that first step toward investing or entrepreneurial action. This requires clarity of goal, accurate risk assessment, the ability to deal with uncertainties, and an understanding of how factors like our level of optimism/pessimism, personal interests, and access to financial resources adjust the equation.

With the right self-awareness, focus, and effort, we can achieve the Financial Independence Mindset, defined as the belief in ourselves that we can provide for ourselves and our families, regardless of circumstances, by leveraging our skill sets and interests to generate income.

At that point, we've earned the luxury of bridging our Passion Gap.

Despite popular belief, passion doesn't have to be reduced to something binary, with only the lucky few—born with either rare top talent or an outsized nest egg—being able to pursue passion while thriving financially.

Here's where the *when* question comes into play. I believe that, with the right strategy and enough time, we can all learn to utilize our interests, aptitudes, unique factors, and operating styles to optimize our skill sets. Next, it all comes down to monetizing this skill set so that we can incorporate our passions into our careers—all while providing financially for ourselves and serving our North Stars.

Reconciling passion with both our need to earn and our core values provides new insight into life's meaning and purpose. When we wake up each morning doing what we love, supporting our preferred lifestyle levels, and serving our primary North Star, life becomes inherently meaningful. We are also now equipped to incorporate "purpose" through our external impact on the world, using those same skill sets and passions toward something beyond ourselves that we care deeply about.

Importantly, this impact doesn't have to be some grand sacrifice or famous deed. In fact, I believe we can all find the right balance—both between values and lifestyle/income, and between meaning and purpose—to live lives full of what Aristotle called *eudaimonia*: lasting happiness.

Now, it's your turn. I hope you get out there and forge your own personal *pursuit of happiness*—the kind that lasts a whole lifetime and then some, echoing throughout every life you enrich along the way.

NOTES

INTRODUCTION

1. Organization for Economic Co-Operation and Development, "Average Annual Hours Actually Worked per Worker," https://stats.oecd.org/index.aspx?DataSetCode=ANHRS.

CHAPTER 1

1. Janine Zacharia, "The Bing 'Marshmallow Studies': 50 Years of Continuing Research," Stanford Bing Nursery School, September 24, 2015, https://bingschool.stanford.edu/news/bing-marshmallow-studies-50-years-continuing-research. However, the study has since been challenged by some. See also, Dee Gill, "New Study Disavows Marshmallow Test's Predictive Powers," UCLA Anderson Review—Feature, February 24, 2021, https://anderson-review.ucla.edu/new-study-disavows-marshmallow-tests-predictive-powers/.

2. Oxford Reference, "Friedrich Nietzsche 1844–1900: German Philosopher and Writer," https://www.oxfordreference.com/display/10.1093/acref/9780191843730.001.0001/q-oro-ed5-00007886.

CHAPTER 2

1. Paula Black, "Live with Purpose: How to Find Your 'North Star,'" *Forbes*, November 12, 2019, https://www.forbes.com/sites/forbescoachescouncil/2019/11/12/live-with-purpose-how-to-find-your-north-star/.

2. Liz Mineo, "Good Genes Are Nice, but Joy Is Better," *Harvard Gazette*, April 11, 2017, https://news.harvard.edu/gazette/story/2017/04/over-nearly-80-years-harvard-study-has-been-showing-how-to-live-a-healthy-and-happy-life/. See also, "Study of Adult Development," Harvard Second Generation Study website, https://www.adultdevelopmentstudy.org/grantandglueckstudy.

3. Martin E. P. Seligman and Ed Royzman, "Authentic Happiness," University of Pennsylvania—Newsletters, July 2003, https://www.authentichappiness.sas.upenn.edu/newsletters/authentichappiness/happiness.

4. Simon Hattenstone, "Angelina Jolie: 'I Just Want My Family to Heal,'" *Guardian*, September 4, 2021, https://www.theguardian.com/film/2021/sep/04/angelina-jolie-i-just-want-my-family-to-heal.

CHAPTER 3

1. Mariko Oi, "Cost of Car Ownership Soars in Singapore," BBC, October 5, 2023, https://www.bbc.com/news/business-67014420.

2. Glenn Firebaugh and Matthew B. Schroeder, "Does Your Neighbor's Income Affect Your Happiness?"

American Journey of Sociology 115, no. 3 (November 2009): 805–831, https://www.journals.uchicago.edu/doi/abs/10.1086/603534?mobileUi=0&.

3. Ed Diener & Robert Biswas-Diener, "Will Money Increase Subjective Well-Being?" *Social Indicators Research* 57 (February 1, 2002): 119–169, doi: 10.1023/A:1014411319119.

4. Andrew T. Jebb et al., "Happiness, Income Satiation and Turning Points around the World," *Nature Human Behaviour* 2 (2018): 33–38, https://doi.org/10.1038/s41562-017-0277-0.

5. Michele W. Berger, "Money Matters to Happiness—Perhaps More than Previously Thought," *Penn Today*, January 18, 2021, https://penntoday.upenn.edu/news/money-matters-to-happiness-perhaps-more-than-previously-thought.

6. Adela Suliman, "Can Money Buy Happiness? Scientists Say It Can," *Washington Post*, March 8, 2023, https://www.washingtonpost.com/business/2023/03/08/money-wealth-happiness-study/.

7. Jeannine Mancini, "Warren Buffett's $31,500 House Is Now Worth $1.4 Million but He Says He Would Have Made Far More Money by Renting Instead," Yahoo! Finance, November 17, 2023, https://finance.yahoo.com/news/warren-buffetts-31-500-house-181400983.html.

8. Jeannine Mancini, "Bill Gates Recalls the Time Warren Buffett Slept Over and He Found Him in the Kitchen Eating Oreos for Breakfast—'It's a Diet that Somehow Works for Him,'" Yahoo! Finance, February 8, 2024, https://finance.yahoo.com/news/bill-gates-recalls-time-warren-163525924.html?fr=sycsrp_catchall.

9. Robert Armstrong, Eric Platt, and Oliver Ralph, "Warren

Buffett: 'I'm Having More Fun than Any 88-Year-Old in the World,'" *Financial Times*, April 25, 2019, https://www.ft.com/content/40b9b356-661e-11e9-a79d-04f350474d62.

CHAPTER 4

1. Anna Baluch, "Average PTO in the US & Other PTO Statistics (2024)," *Forbes Advisor*, March 30, 2023, https://www.forbes.com/advisor/business/pto-statistics/.

2. Urban Institute and Brookings Institution, "Historical Highest Marginal Income Tax Rates," Tax Policy Center, May 11, 2023, https://www.taxpolicycenter.org/statistics/historical-highest-marginal-income-tax-rates.

3. Mark Olfson et al., "National Trends in the Outpatient Treatment of Depression," *JAMA* 287, no. 2 (January 9, 2002): 203–209, doi: 10.1001/jama.287.2.203.

4. "Unemployment and Mental Health," Institute for Work & Health, August 2009, https://www.iwh.on.ca/plain-language-summaries/unemployment-and-mental-health.

5. Juliet B. Schor, *The Overspent American: Why We Want What We Don't Need* (New York: Harper Perennial, 1999), 22.

6. Janna Koretz, "What Happens When Your Career Becomes Your Whole Identity," *Harvard Business Review*, December 26, 2019, https://hbr.org/2019/12/what-happens-when-your-career-becomes-your-whole-identity.

7. Sander van't Noordende, "How Working Patterns Are Changing around the World," World Economic Forum—Davos Agenda, January 19,

2023, https://www.weforum.org/agenda/2023/01/how-working-patterns-are-changing-around-the-world/.

8. Shawn Achor et al., "9 Out of 10 People Are Willing to Earn Less Money to Do More-Meaningful Work," *Harvard Business Review*, November 6, 2018, https://hbr.org/2018/11/9-out-of-10-people-are-willing-to-earn-less-money-to-do-more-meaningful-work.

9. "Business Roundtable Redefines the Purpose of a Corporation to Promote 'An Economy that Serves All Americans,'" Business Roundtable, August 19, 2019, https://www.businessroundtable.org/business-roundtable-redefines-the-purpose-of-a-corporation-to-promote-an-economy-that-serves-all-americans.

10. Anna Jasinenko and Josephina Steuber, "Perceived Organizational Purpose: Systematic Literature Review, Construct Definition, Measurement and Potential Employee Outcomes," *Journal of Management Studies* 60, no. 6 (September 2023): 1415–1447, doi:10.1111/joms.12852.

11. Jasinenko and Steuber, "Perceived Organizational Purpose."

CHAPTER 5

1. Sean Fleming, "Top 10 Tech Trends that Will Shape the Coming Decade, According to McKinsey," World Economic Forum—Emerging Technologies, October 12, 2021, https://www.weforum.org/agenda/2021/10/technology-trends-top-10-mckinsey/.

2. World Economic Forum, *Future of Jobs Report 2023*,

April 30, 2023, https://www.weforum.org/publications/the-future-of-jobs-report-2023/.

3. James Manyika et al., "Jobs Lost, Jobs Gained: Workforce Transitions in a time of Automation—Executive Summary," McKinsey Global Institute, December 2017, https://www.mckinsey.com/~/media/mckinsey/industries/public%20and%20social%20sector/our%20insights/what%20the%20future%20of%20work%20will%20mean%20for%20jobs%20skills%20and%20wages/mgi-jobs-lost-jobs-gained-executive-summary-december-6-2017.pdf.

4. David Crouch, "Is Sweden the Best Place to Lose Your Job?," December 19, 2019, https://www.bbc.com/worklife/article/20191212-where-losing-your-job-is-a-good-thing.

5. Bureau of Labor Statistics, "Employee Tenure in 2022," United States Department of Labor, September 22, 2022, https://www.bls.gov/news.release/pdf/tenure.pdf.

6. Chris Kolmar, "Average Number of Jobs in a Lifetime [2023]: How Many Jobs Does the Average Person Have," Zippia, January 11, 2023, https://www.zippia.com/advice/average-number-jobs-in-lifetime/#:~:text=Millennials%20stay%20at%20their%20jobs,and%2034%20is%202.8%20years.

7. "American Worklife," NPR/Marist National Poll, January 23, 2018, https://maristpoll.marist.edu/polls/123-picture-of-work-in-the-united-states/.

8. Kweilin Ellingrud, "Meet the US Workers Who Are Going It Alone—and Feeling Good about It," McKinsey Global Institute, November 1, 2022, https://www.mckinsey.com/mgi/overview/in-the-news/meet-the-us-workers-who-are-going-it-alone.

9. Intuit, *Intuit 2020 Report: Twenty Trends that Will Shape the Next Decade*, https://http-download.intuit.com/http.intuit/CMO/intuit/futureofsmallbusiness/intuit_2020_report.pdf.

10. Josh Bivens and Jori Kandra, "CEO Pay Slightly Declined in 2022," Economic Policy Institute, September 21, 2023, https://www.epi.org/publication/ceo-pay-in-2022.

CHAPTER 6

1. Bing Feng et al., "Why Do People Fail to Act on Financial Plans? A Behavioural Lens on Financial Planning," October 10, 2019. White paper given at Behavioral Economics in Action at Rotman (Toronto, Canada), https://static1.squarespace.com/static/5d1e3407108c4a0001f99a0f/t/5db7263ff3cffa7787918198/1572283968543/BEAR-FinancialPlanning-1.pdf.

2. Fazelina Sahul Hamid et al., "Determinants of Financial Resilience: Insights from an Emerging Economy," *Journal of Social and Economic Development* 25 (March 2023): 479–499, https://link.springer.com/article/10.1007/s40847-023-00239-y.

CHAPTER 7

1. Warren E. Buffett to Berkshire Hathaway Inc., February 26, 2022, https://www.berkshirehathaway.com/letters/2021ltr.pdf.

2. Marcel Schwantes, "Warren Buffett Says This Is What Makes Him Jump Out of Bed Excited Every Morning (at the Age of 88)," *Inc.*, April 30, 2019, https://www.inc.com/

marcel-schwantes/warren-buffett-says-this-is-what-makes-him-jump-out-of-bed-excited-every-morning-at-age-of-88.html.

3. Simon Sinek, "Working Hard for Something We," X/Twitter, February 28, 2012, https://twitter.com/simonsinek/status/174469085726375936?lang=en.

4. Catherine Clifford, "Billionaire Mark Cuban: 'One of the Great Lies of Life Is Follow Your Passions,'" CNBC, February 19, 2018, https://www.cnbc.com/2018/02/16/mark-cuban-follow-your-passion-is-bad-advice.html.

5. Courtney Connley, "Mike Rowe of 'Dirty Jobs' Says 'Follow Your Passion' Is Bad Advice—Here's What to Do Instead," CNBC, December 6, 2018, https://www.cnbc.com/2018/12/06/mike-rowe-of-dirty-jobs-says-follow-opportunity-not-passion.html.

CHAPTER 8

1. "Top 101 Most Inspiring Quotes on Money (Wealthy)," Gracious Quotes, December 28, 2023, https://graciousquotes.com/money-quotes.

CHAPTER 9

1. Kunal Singh, "5 Steps for Finding Your Purpose in Life," *Thrive Global*, August 26, 2021, https://community.thriveglobal.com/5-steps-for-finding-your-purpose-in-life/.

ABOUT THE AUTHOR

PHILIP HSIN and his family fled Phnom Penh, Cambodia, just days before its fall to the Khmer Rouge. The first Cambodian refugee family to arrive in Portland, Oregon, they relied on government aid until his parents could begin working. After more than three decades spent in the corporate world, Philip is now focused on spending time with his two young children and on his passion projects.

He was most recently a managing director at PGIM, one of the largest global asset management firms. He also held senior positions at Capital International, Barclays Global Investors, and Goldman Sachs Asset Management. He earned a BS degree in finance with a minor in behavioral sciences from Oregon State University and an executive MBA degree from the Kellogg School of Management at Northwestern University and the Hong Kong University of Science and Technology. Philip is also a member of the Panel of Community Advisors to Honour (Singapore), a nonprofit organization dedicated to promoting a culture of honor and honorable behavior for the well-being of Singapore.

Milton Keynes UK
Ingram Content Group UK Ltd.
UKHW041316121224
3635UKWH00008B/12/J